CREATIVE
HOME COOKING

CREATIVE HOME COOKING

FRANCES CLEARY

Dolphin Publications

This edition specially produced for
Dolphin Publications,
Bridge Mills Business Park,
Langley Road South
Pendleton
Salford, M6 6EL

First published by Dolphin Publications in 1993
and exclusive to them in the UK.

© 1993 Anness Publishing Limited
Boundary Row Studios
1 Boundary Row
London SE1 8HP

ISBN 1-873762-61-5

Editorial Director: Joanna Lorenz
Project Editor: Carole Clements
Copy Editors: Norma MacMillan and Penny David
Designer: Sheila Volpe
Photographer: Amanda Heywood
Food Styling: Frances Cleary, Carole Handslip,
steps by Nicola Fowler

Printed and bound in Hong Kong

Contents

~

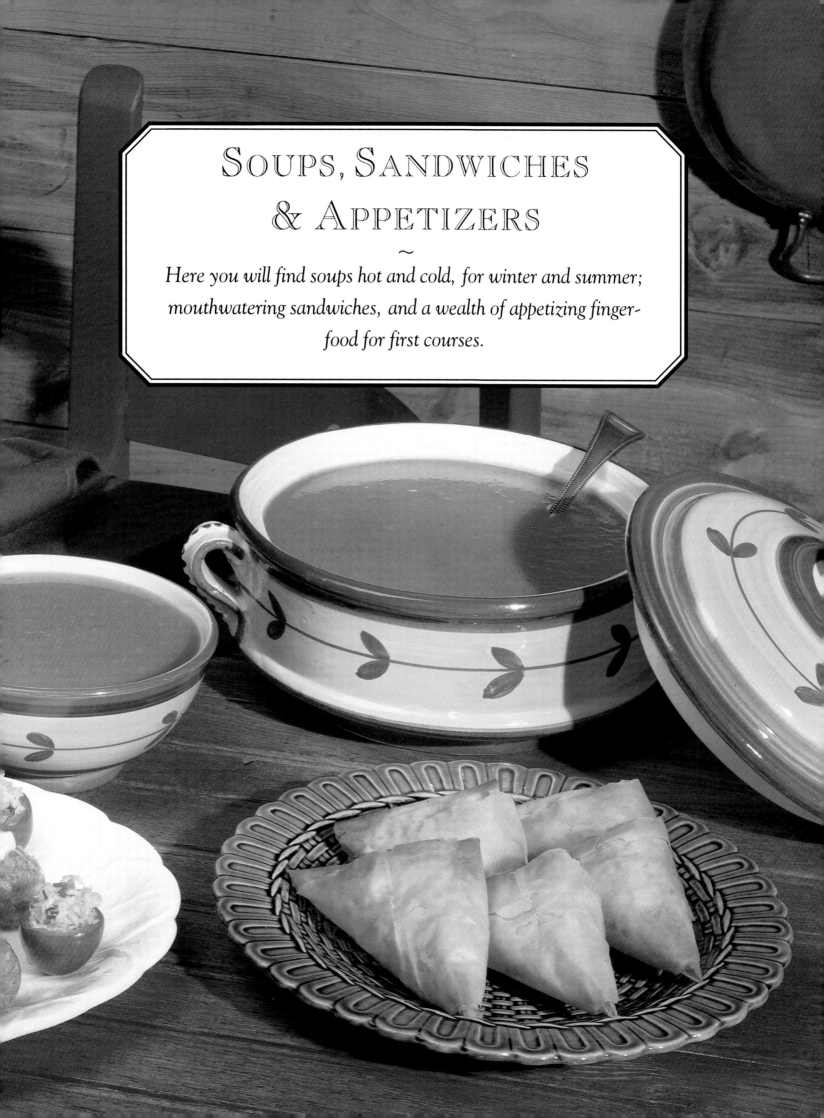

Soups, Sandwiches & Appetizers

~

Here you will find soups hot and cold, for winter and summer;
mouthwatering sandwiches, and a wealth of appetizing finger-
food for first courses.

Warming Winter Vegetable Soup

SERVES 8

1 medium-size head of Savoy cabbage, quartered and cored

2 tbsp vegetable oil

4 carrots, thinly sliced

2 celery sticks, thinly sliced

2 parsnips, diced

2½ pt (1.5 litres) chicken stock

3 medium-size potatoes, diced

2 courgettes, sliced

1 small red pepper, seeded and diced

1 small cauliflower, stems trimmed and separated into florets

2 tomatoes, seeded and diced

½ tsp fresh thyme leaves, or ¼ tsp dried thyme

2 tbsp chopped fresh parsley

salt and pepper

1 Slice the cabbage quarters into thin strips across the leaves.

2 ▲ Heat the oil in a large saucepan. Add the cabbage, carrots, celery and parsnips and cook 10–15 minutes over medium heat, stirring frequently.

3 Stir the stock into the vegetables and bring to the boil. Skim off any foam that rises to the top.

4 ▲ Add the potatoes, courgettes, pepper, cauliflower and tomatoes with the herbs, and salt and pepper to taste. Bring back to the boil. Reduce the heat to low, cover the pan, and simmer until the vegetables are tender, 15–20 minutes.

Traditional Tomato Soup

SERVES 4

1 oz (30 g) butter or margarine

1 onion, chopped

2 lb (900 g) tomatoes, quartered

2 carrots, chopped

16 fl oz (500 ml) chicken stock

2 tbsp chopped fresh parsley

½ tsp fresh thyme leaves, or ¼ tsp dried thyme

3 fl oz (85 ml) whipping cream (optional)

salt and pepper

~ **COOK'S TIP** ~

Canned Italian plum tomatoes are ideal for this soup.

1 Melt the butter or margarine in a large saucepan. Add the onion and cook until softened, about 5 minutes.

2 ▲ Stir in the tomatoes, carrots, chicken stock, parsley and thyme. Bring to the boil. Reduce the heat to low, cover the pan, and simmer until tender, 15–20 minutes.

3 ▼ Purée the soup in a vegetable mill. Return the puréed soup to the saucepan.

4 Stir in the cream, if using, and reheat gently. Season with salt and pepper. Ladle into warmed soup bowls and serve hot, sprinkled with a little more thyme, if you wish.

Warming Winter Vegetable Soup (top), Traditional Tomato Soup

Chilled Avocado and Courgette Soup

Serves 6

1¾ pt (1 litre) chicken stock

1 lb (450 g) courgettes, sliced

2 large, very ripe avocados

3 tbsp fresh lemon juice

6 fl oz (175 ml) plain yogurt

2 tsp Worcestershire sauce

½ tsp chilli powder

⅛ tsp sugar

dash of chilli sauce

salt

1 In a large saucepan, bring the chicken stock to the boil.

2 ▲ Add the courgettes and simmer until soft, 10–15 minutes. Let cool.

3 ▲ Peel the avocados. Remove and discard the stones. Cut the flesh into chunks and put in a food processor or blender. Add the lemon juice and process until smooth.

4 ▲ Using a slotted spoon, transfer the courgettes to the food processor or blender; reserve the stock. Process the courgettes with the avocado purée.

5 ▲ Pour the avocado-courgette purée into a bowl. Stir in the reserved stock. Add two-thirds of the yogurt, the Worcestershire sauce, chilli powder, sugar, chilli sauce and salt to taste. Mix well. Cover tightly and chill 3–4 hours.

6 To serve, ladle the soup into bowls. Swirl the remaining yogurt on the surface.

Chicken Soup with Noodles

SERVES 8

1 × 3 lb (1.35 kg) chicken, cut in pieces
2 onions, quartered
1 parsnip, quartered
2 carrots, quartered
½ tsp salt
1 bay leaf
2 allspice berries
4 black peppercorns
4¾ pt (3 litres) water
3 oz (85 g) very thin egg noodles
sprigs of fresh dill, for garnishing

1 ▲ In a large saucepan, combine the chicken pieces, onions, parsnip, carrots, salt, bay leaf, allspice berries and peppercorns.

2 ▲ Add the water to the pan and bring to the boil, skimming frequently.

3 Reduce the heat to low and simmer 1½ hours, skimming occasionally.

4 Strain the broth through a fine-mesh strainer into a bowl. Cool then refrigerate overnight.

5 ▲ When the chicken pieces are cool enough to handle, remove the meat from the bones. Discard the bones, skin, vegetables and flavourings. Chop the chicken meat and refrigerate overnight.

6 Remove the solidified fat from the surface of the chilled broth. Pour the broth into a saucepan and bring to the boil. Taste the broth; if a more concentrated flavour is wanted, boil 10 minutes to reduce slightly.

7 ▲ Add the chicken meat and noodles to the broth and cook until the noodles are tender, about 8 minutes (check packet instructions for timing). Serve hot, garnished with dill sprigs.

Green Bean Soup with Parmesan Cheese

SERVES 4

1 oz (30 g) butter or margarine

8 oz (225 g) green beans, trimmed

1 garlic clove, crushed

16 fl oz (500 ml) vegetable stock

salt and pepper

2 oz (55 g) Parmesan cheese

2 fl oz (65 ml) single cream

2 tbsp chopped fresh parsley

1 Melt the butter or margarine in a medium saucepan. Add the green beans and garlic and cook 2–3 minutes over medium heat, stirring frequently.

2 ▲ Stir in the stock and season with salt and pepper. Bring to the boil. Reduce the heat and simmer, uncovered, until the beans are tender, 10–15 minutes.

3 ▼ Pour the soup into a blender or food processor and process until smooth. Alternatively, purée the soup in a food mill. Return to the pan. Stir in the grated cheese and cream. Sprinkle with the parsley and serve.

Hearty Lentil Soup

SERVES 6

6 oz (175 g) brown lentils

1¾ pt (1 litre) chicken stock

8 fl oz (250 ml) water

2 fl oz (65 ml) dry red wine

1½ lb (700 g) ripe tomatoes, peeled, seeded and chopped, or 14 oz (400 g) canned chopped tomatoes

1 carrot, sliced

1 onion, chopped

1 celery stick, sliced

1 garlic clove, crushed

¼ tsp ground coriander

2 tsp chopped fresh basil, or ½ tsp dried basil

1 bay leaf

6 tbsp freshly grated Parmesan cheese

1 ▲ Rinse the lentils and discard any discoloured ones and any grit.

2 ▲ Combine the lentils, stock, water, wine, tomatoes, carrot, onion, celery and garlic in a large saucepan. Add the coriander, basil and bay leaf.

3 ▼ Bring to the boil, reduce the heat to low, cover and simmer until the lentils are just tender, 20–25 minutes, stirring occasionally.

4 Discard the bay leaf. Ladle the soup into 6 soup bowls and sprinkle each with 1 tablespoon of the cheese.

~ **VARIATION** ~

For a more substantial soup, add about 4 oz (115 g) finely chopped cooked ham for the last 10 minutes of cooking.

Green Bean Soup with Parmesan Cheese (top), Hearty Lentil Soup

Mozzarella Cheese and Tomato Sandwiches

SERVES 4

4 small round white bread rolls

4 fl oz (125 ml) freshly made or bottled pesto sauce

8 oz (225 g) Mozzarella cheese, thinly sliced

4 medium tomatoes, thinly sliced

3 tbsp olive oil

fresh basil leaves, for garnishing

1 With a serrated knife, cut each roll open in half. Spread 1 tablespoon of pesto sauce over the cut side of each half.

2 ▲ Arrange alternating slices of Mozzarella cheese and tomato on the bottom half of each roll.

3 ▲ Drizzle the olive oil over the cheese and tomatoes.

4 Replace the top half of each roll; garnish with basil leaves, if you wish.

Greek Salad in Pitta Bread

SERVES 6

½ small head of iceberg lettuce, cut in fine strips across the leaves

½ cucumber, diced

9 cherry tomatoes, halved

2 spring onions, finely chopped

4 oz (115 g) feta cheese, crumbled

8 black olives, stoned and chopped

6 oval pitta breads, cut in half crosswise

FOR THE DRESSING

1 small garlic clove, crushed

⅛ tsp salt

1 tsp fresh lemon juice

2 tbsp olive oil

1 tsp chopped fresh mint

pepper

1 ▲ In a bowl, combine the lettuce, cucumber, tomatoes, spring onions, feta cheese and olives.

2 ▲ For the dressing, combine all the ingredients in a small screwtop jar and shake well to mix.

3 ▲ Pour the dressing over the salad and toss together.

4 ▲ Gently open the pitta bread halves. Fill the pockets with the salad. Serve immediately.

Mozzarella Cheese and Tomato Sandwiches (top), Greek Salad in Pitta Bread

Club Sandwiches

Serves 4

8 rashers of bacon

12 slices of white bread, toasted

4 fl oz (125 ml) mayonnaise

4–8 oz (115–225 g) cooked chicken breast meat, sliced

8 large lettuce leaves

salt and pepper

1 beef tomato, cut across in 4 slices

1 ▼ In a heavy frying pan, fry the bacon until crisp and the fat is rendered. Drain on kitchen paper.

2 Lay 4 slices of toast on a flat surface. Spread them with some of the mayonnaise.

3 ▲ Top each slice with one-quarter of the chicken and a lettuce leaf. Season with salt and pepper.

4 ▲ Spread 4 of the remaining toast slices with mayonnaise. Lay them on top of the lettuce.

5 ▲ Top each sandwich with a slice of tomato, 2 rashers of bacon and another lettuce leaf.

6 Spread the remaining slices of toast with the rest of the mayonnaise. Place them on top of the sandwiches, mayonnaise-side down.

7 Cut each sandwich into 4 triangles and secure each triangle with a cocktail stick.

Chilli Hot Dogs

Serves 6

6 frankfurters

6 large finger rolls, split open

1 oz (30 g) butter or margarine

1½ oz (45 g) Cheddar cheese, grated

1½ oz (45 g) red onion, chopped

For the chilli

2 tbsp corn oil

1 small onion, chopped

½ green pepper, seeded and chopped

8 oz (225 g) minced beef

8 fl oz (250 ml) fresh tomatoes, blanched, skinned, cooked and sieved

3 oz (85 g) drained canned red kidney beans

2 tsp chilli powder, or to taste

salt and pepper

3 ▼ Stir in the sieved tomatoes, beans, chilli powder and salt and pepper to taste. Cover the pan and simmer 10 minutes.

4 Meanwhile, put the frankfurters in a saucepan and cover with cold water. Bring to the boil. Remove from the heat, cover and let stand 5 minutes.

5 ▲ Spread both sides of each finger roll with the butter or margarine. Fry in a hot frying pan until golden brown on both sides.

6 To serve, put a frankfurter in each bun. Top with chilli and sprinkle with cheese and onion. Serve immediately.

1 ▲ For the chilli, heat the oil in a frying pan. Add the onion and green pepper and cook until softened, about 5 minutes.

2 ▲ Add the beef and cook until well browned, stirring frequently and breaking up lumps with the side of a wooden spatula.

Cheese and Spinach Pastry Delights

SERVES 20

2 tbsp olive oil

2 shallots or 1 small onion, finely chopped

1 lb (450 g) frozen spinach, thawed

4 oz (115 g) feta cheese, crumbled

2 oz (55 g) chopped walnuts

¼ tsp grated nutmeg

salt and pepper

4 large sheets frozen filo pastry, thawed

4 oz (115 g) butter or margarine, melted

1 Preheat a 400°F/200°C/Gas 6 oven.

2 ▲ Heat the olive oil in a frying pan. Add the shallots or onion and cook until softened, about 5 minutes.

3 ▲ A handful at a time, squeeze all the liquid out of the spinach. Add the spinach to the shallots or onion. Increase the heat to high and cook, stirring, until all excess moisture has evaporated, about 5 minutes.

4 ▲ Transfer the spinach mixture to a bowl. Let cool. Stir in the feta and walnuts. Season with nutmeg, salt and pepper.

5 ▲ Lay a filo sheet on a flat surface. (Keep the remaining filo covered with a damp tea towel to prevent it drying out.) Brush with some of the butter or margarine. Lay a second filo sheet on top of the first. With scissors, cut the layered filo pastry lengthwise into 3 in (8 cm) wide strips.

~ **VARIATION** ~

For an alternative filling, omit the spinach and shallots. Use 12 oz (350 g) crumbled goat cheese, instead of the feta cheese, and 2 oz (55 g) toasted pine kernels instead of the walnuts. Mix the cheese with the olive oil and 1 tablespoon chopped fresh basil.

6 ▲ Place a tablespoonful of the spinach mixture at the end of one strip of filo pastry.

7 ▲ Fold a bottom corner of the pastry over the filling to form a triangle, then continue folding over the pastry strip to the other end. Fill and shape the triangles until all the ingredients are used.

8 ▲ Set the triangles on baking sheets and brush with butter. Bake the filo triangles until they are crispy and golden brown, about 10 minutes. Serve hot.

Smoked Salmon Buns

MAKES 25

2 oz (55 g) cornmeal or polenta

1 oz (30 g) plain flour

½ tsp baking powder

⅛ tsp salt

1 tbsp sugar

1 egg

4 fl oz (125 ml) buttermilk

2 fl oz (65 ml) single cream

2½ oz (70 g) smoked salmon, cut in fine strips

1 Preheat a 400°F/200°C/Gas 6 oven. Grease 1–2 small bun trays.

2 In a mixing bowl, combine the cornmeal, flour, baking powder, salt and sugar. Set aside.

3 ▼ In another bowl, mix together the egg, buttermilk and cream. Gradually add the egg mixture to the cornmeal mixture, stirring quickly until just combined.

4 ▲ Stir the smoked salmon strips into the bun mixture.

5 Fill the small bun trays three-quarters full with the bun mixture. Bake until slightly risen and golden brown, 18–20 minutes. Let cool 5 minutes in the trays on a wire rack before unmoulding.

Spicy Mexican Snack Cups

MAKES 30

14 oz (400 g) canned black or red kidney beans, rinsed and drained

2 tomatoes, seeded and diced

1 garlic clove, crushed

1 shallot or ½ small onion, minced

1 chilli pepper, seeded and chopped

1 tsp finely grated lime or lemon rind

1 tbsp olive oil

2 tbsp fresh lime or lemon juice

2 tsp maple syrup

salt and pepper

3 tbsp chopped fresh coriander

FOR THE CUPS

10 × 6 in (15 cm) corn tortillas

3–4 tbsp corn oil, for brushing

1 Preheat a 400°F/200°C/Gas 6 oven.

2 ▼ For the cups, using a 2 in (5 cm) round pastry cutter, cut 3 rounds from each tortilla, pressing firmly to cut through. Discard the tortilla trimmings. Brush both sides of each tortilla round with oil.

3 Press the tortilla rounds into small bun trays. Bake until crisp, about 6 minutes. Let cool on a wire rack.

4 ▲ In a mixing bowl, combine the beans, tomatoes, garlic, shallot or onion, chilli pepper, lime rind, oil, lime juice and maple syrup. Stir in salt and pepper to taste.

5 Place a spoonful of the bean and tomato mixture in each cup. Sprinkle with the chopped coriander just before serving.

Smoked Salmon Buns (top), Spicy Mexican Snack Cups

Potato Pancakes with a Tangy Dip

MAKES 40

2 tbsp butter or margarine

1 shallot, finely chopped

1 egg

8 oz (225 g) potatoes

salt and pepper

oil for frying

FOR THE DIP

4 oz (115 g) cream cheese

2 tbsp soured cream

1 tsp finely grated lemon rind

1 tbsp fresh lemon juice

1 tbsp chopped fresh chives

1 Melt the butter or margarine in a small frying pan. Add the shallot and cook until softened, about 3 minutes. Set aside and let cool.

2 Beat the egg in a large mixing bowl until light and frothy.

3 Coarsely grate the potatoes. Add them to the bowl and mix with the egg until completely coated. Season generously with salt and pepper. Add the shallot and mix well.

4 ▼ For the tangy dip, combine the cream cheese and soured cream in a bowl. Beat until smooth. Add the lemon rind and juice and the chives. Set aside.

5 ▲ Heat ¼ in (5 mm) of oil in a frying pan. Drop teaspoonfuls of the potato mixture into the hot oil and press them with the back of a spoon to make flat rounds. Fry until well browned, 2–3 minutes on each side. Drain on kitchen paper and keep warm. Fry the remaining pancakes.

6 Serve the pancakes hot, with the dip either spooned on top or served in a separate bowl.

Cherry Tomatoes Stuffed with Crab

MAKES 40

4 oz (115 g) crab meat

1 tsp chilli sauce

¼ tsp Dijon mustard

2 tbsp mayonnaise

½ tsp Worcestershire sauce

2 spring onions, finely chopped

1 tbsp chopped fresh basil

1 tbsp chopped fresh chives

40 cherry tomatoes

salt

1 In a mixing bowl, combine the crab meat, chilli sauce, mustard, mayonnaise, Worcestershire sauce, spring onions and herbs. Mix well. Cover and refrigerate until needed.

2 ▲ Using a serrated knife, cut a very thin slice from the stem end of each tomato. Carefully scoop out the pulp and seeds with the tip of a teaspoon.

3 Sprinkle the insides of the tomato shells lightly with salt. Invert them on kitchen paper and let them drain 15 minutes.

4 ▲ Using a small spoon, stuff the tomatoes with the crab, mounding the filling slightly on top. Serve cold.

Potato Pancakes with a Tangy Dip (top), Cherry Tomatoes Stuffed with Crab

Sweetcorn Fritters

SERVES 4

5 garlic cloves

3 eggs, beaten

3 oz (85 g) plain flour

salt and pepper

6 oz (175 g) drained canned sweetcorn, or frozen sweetcorn, thawed

8 fl oz (250 ml) soured cream

2 tbsp chopped fresh chives

3 tbsp corn oil

1 Preheat the grill.

2 Thread the garlic cloves onto a skewer. Grill close to the heat, turning, until charred and soft. Let cool.

3 ▼ Peel the garlic cloves. Place them in a bowl and mash with a fork. Add the eggs, flour and salt and pepper to taste and stir until well mixed. Stir in the sweetcorn. Set aside for at least 30 minutes.

4 In a small bowl, combine the soured cream and chives. Cover and refrigerate.

5 ▲ To cook the fritters, heat the oil in a frying pan. Drop in spoonfuls of the batter and fry until lightly browned on both sides, about 2 minutes, turning once. Drain on kitchen paper.

6 Serve the fritters hot with the chive dip.

Cheese and Mushroom Open Omelette

SERVES 4

2 tbsp olive oil

4 oz (115 g) small mushrooms, sliced

3 spring onions, finely chopped

6 eggs

4 oz (115 g) Cheddar cheese, grated

1 tbsp chopped fresh dill, or ¼ tsp dried dill

salt and pepper

1 Heat the oil in a heavy 8 in (20 cm) frying pan, preferably with an ovenproof handle. Add the mushrooms and spring onions and cook over medium heat until wilted, about 3 minutes, stirring occasionally.

2 ▲ Break the eggs into a bowl and beat to mix. Add the cheese, dill and salt and pepper to taste.

3 Preheat the grill.

4 ▼ Spread the vegetables evenly in the frying pan. Pour the egg mixture over them. Cook until the omelette is set at the edge, and the underside is golden, 5–6 minutes.

5 Place the frying pan under the grill, about 3 in (8 cm) from the heat. Grill until the top has set and is lightly browned, 3–4 minutes. Transfer to a warmed platter for serving.

Sweetcorn Fritters (top), Cheese and Mushroom Open Omelette

Baked Potatoes with Cheesy Topping

MAKES 20

20 small new potatoes

2 fl oz (65 ml) vegetable oil

coarse salt

4 fl oz (125 ml) soured cream

1 oz (30 g) blue cheese, crumbled

2 tbsp chopped fresh chives

1 Preheat a 350°F/180°C/Gas 4 oven.

2 Wash and dry the potatoes. Pour the oil into a bowl. Add the potatoes and toss to coat well with oil.

3 ▼ Dip the potatoes in the coarse salt to coat lightly. Spread out the potatoes on a baking sheet. Bake until tender, 45–50 minutes.

4 ▲ In a small bowl, combine the soured cream and blue cheese.

5 ▲ Cut a cross in the top of each potato. Press with your fingers to open the potatoes.

6 ▲ Top each potato with a dollop of the cheese mixture. Sprinkle with chives and serve immediately.

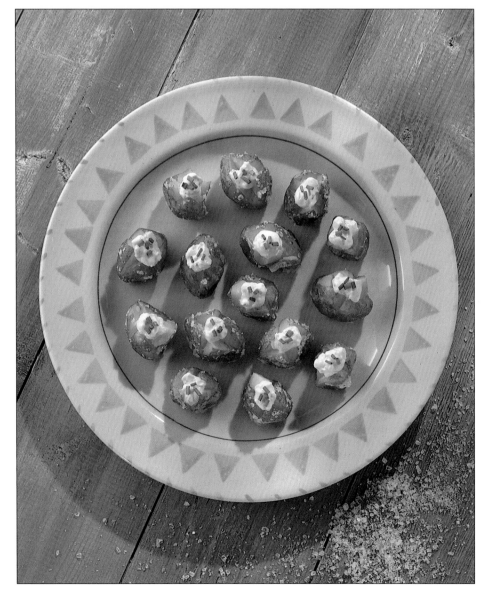

Avocado Dip with Spicy Tortilla Chips

SERVES 10

2 very ripe avocados

2 shallots or spring onions, chopped

2 tbsp fresh lime juice

1 tsp salt

2 tsp chilli powder

1 medium-size tomato, seeded and chopped

FOR THE TORTILLA CHIPS

3 tbsp corn oil

1½ tsp ground cumin

1 tsp salt

9 × 6 in (15 cm) corn tortillas, each cut in 6 triangles

1 Preheat a 300°F/150°C/Gas 2 oven.

2 ▲ For the tortilla chips, combine the oil, cumin and salt in a bowl.

3 ▲ Spread the tortilla triangles on 2 baking sheets. Brush the seasoned oil on both sides. Bake until they are crisp and golden, about 20 minutes, turning once or twice and brushing with the seasoned oil. Let cool.

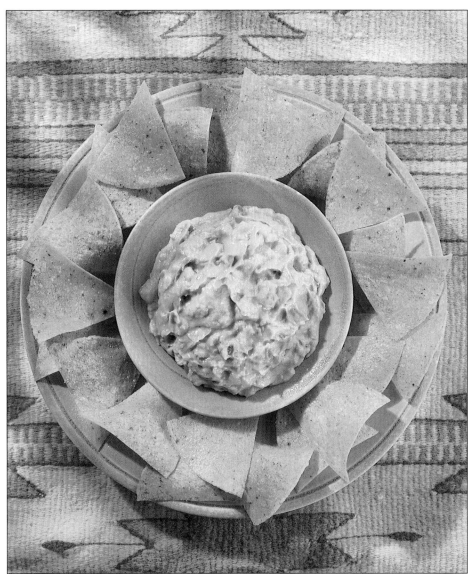

4 ▼ Peel the avocados, discard the stones, and chop the flesh. In a food processor or blender, combine the avocados, shallots or spring onions, lime juice, salt and chilli powder. Process until smooth.

5 ▲ Transfer the mixture to a bowl. Gently stir in the chopped tomato.

6 Serve the avocado dip in a bowl in the centre of a platter, surrounded with the tortilla chips.

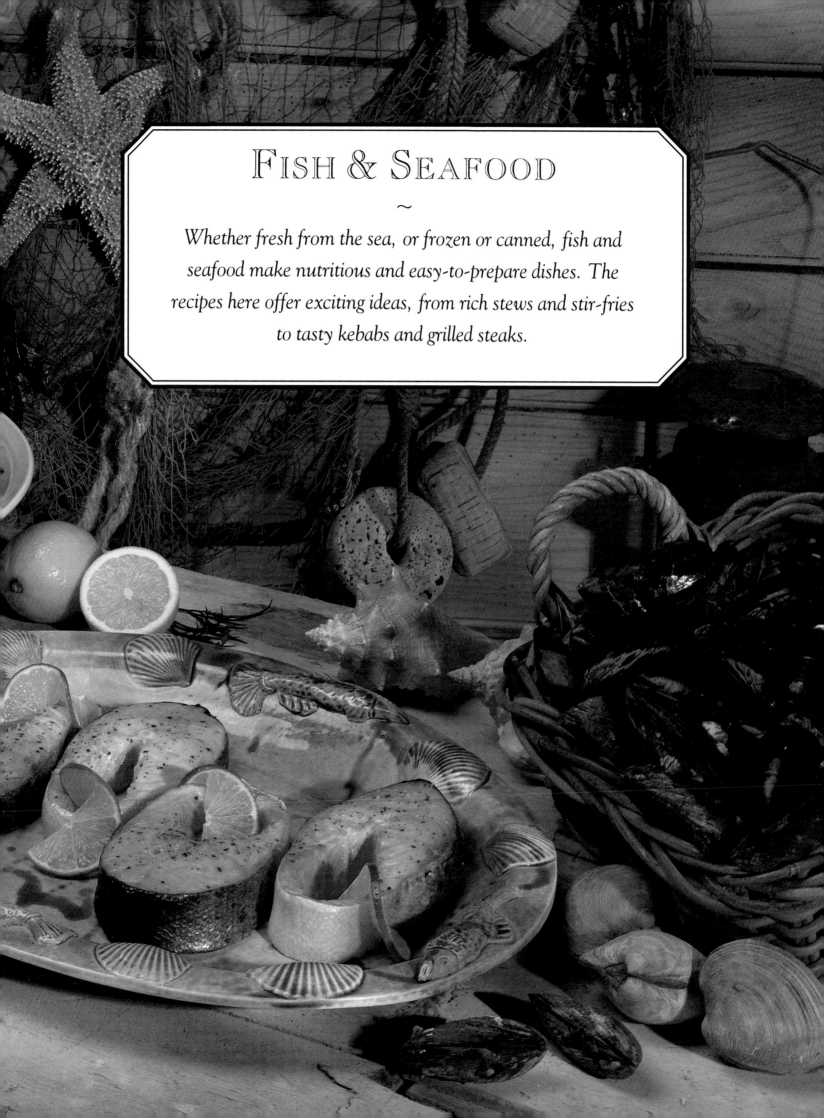

FISH & SEAFOOD

~

Whether fresh from the sea, or frozen or canned, fish and seafood make nutritious and easy-to-prepare dishes. The recipes here offer exciting ideas, from rich stews and stir-fries to tasty kebabs and grilled steaks.

Breaded Fish with Tartare Sauce

SERVES 4

2 oz (55 g) dry breadcrumbs

1 tsp dried oregano

½ tsp cayenne pepper

8 fl oz (250 ml) milk

2 tsp salt

4 pieces of cod fillet (about 1½ lb/ 700 g)

1½ oz (45 g) butter or margarine, melted

FOR THE TARTARE SAUCE

4 fl oz (125 ml) mayonnaise

½ tsp Dijon mustard

1–2 pickled gherkins, finely chopped

1 tbsp drained capers, chopped

1 tsp chopped fresh parsley

1 tsp chopped fresh chives

1 tsp chopped fresh tarragon

salt and pepper

1 Preheat a 450°F/230°C/Gas 8 oven. Grease a shallow ovenproof baking dish.

2 ▲ Combine the breadcrumbs, oregano and cayenne on a plate and blend together. Mix the milk with the salt in a bowl, stirring well to dissolve the salt.

3 ▲ Dip the pieces of cod fillet in the milk, then transfer to the plate and coat with the breadcrumb mixture.

4 ▲ Arrange the coated fish in the prepared baking dish, in one layer. Drizzle the melted butter or margarine over the fish.

5 Bake until the fish flakes easily when tested with a fork, about 10–15 minutes.

6 ▲ Meanwhile, for the tartare sauce, combine all the ingredients in a small bowl. Stir gently to mix well.

7 Serve the fish hot, accompanied by the tartare sauce.

Stuffed Sole

SERVES 4

8 skinless sole fillets (about 1 lb/450 g)
½ oz (15 g) butter or margarine, cut into 8 pieces
2 fl oz (65 ml) dry white wine
paprika, for garnishing
FOR THE STUFFING
1 oz (30 g) butter or margarine
1 small onion, finely chopped
1 handful of fresh spinach leaves, shredded
2 tbsp pine kernels, toasted
2 tbsp raisins
2 tbsp fresh breadcrumbs
⅛ tsp ground cinnamon
salt and pepper

1 Preheat a 400°F/200°C/Gas 6 oven. Butter a shallow baking dish.

2 ▲ For the stuffing, melt the butter or margarine in a small saucepan. Add the onion and cook over medium heat until softened, about 5 minutes. Stir in the spinach and cook, stirring constantly, until the spinach wilts and renders its liquid.

~ **VARIATION** ~

Use plaice instead of sole in this recipe, or try stuffing fillets of lean freshwater fish such as trout or perch.

3 Add the pine kernels, raisins, breadcrumbs, cinnamon and a little salt and pepper. Raise the heat and cook until most of the liquid has evaporated, stirring constantly. Remove from the heat.

4 ▲ Sprinkle the sole fillets with salt and pepper. Place a spoonful of the spinach stuffing at one end of each fillet. Roll up and secure with a wooden cocktail stick, if necessary.

5 ▲ Place the sole rolls in the prepared baking dish. Put a small piece of butter or margarine on each roll. Pour the wine over the fish. Cover the baking dish with foil and bake until the fish flakes easily when tested with a fork, about 15 minutes.

6 Serve on warmed plates with a little of the cooking juices spooned over the fish. Garnish with paprika, if wished.

Grilled Salmon with Lime Butter

SERVES 4

4 salmon steaks (about 1½ lb/700 g)

salt and pepper

FOR THE LIME BUTTER

2 oz (55 g) butter or margarine, at room temperature

1 tbsp chopped fresh coriander, or 1 tsp dried coriander

1 tsp finely grated lime rind

1 tbsp fresh lime juice

1 For the lime butter, combine the butter or margarine, coriander and lime rind and juice in a bowl. Mix well with a fork.

2 ▲ Transfer the lime butter to a piece of greaseproof paper and shape into a log. Roll in the paper until smooth and round. Refrigerate until firm, about 1 hour.

3 Preheat the grill.

4 ▼ Sprinkle the salmon steaks with salt and pepper. Arrange them on the rack in the grill pan. Grill about 3 in (8 cm) from the heat, 5 minutes on each side.

5 Unwrap the lime butter and cut into 4 pieces. Top each salmon steak with a pat of lime butter and serve.

Fish Fillets with Citrus Sauce

SERVES 6

½–1 oz (15–30 g) butter or margarine, melted

2 lb (900 g) sole fillets

salt and pepper

1 tsp grated lemon rind

1 tsp grated orange rind

2 tbsp fresh orange juice

3 fl oz (85 ml) whipping cream

1 tbsp chopped fresh basil

fresh basil sprigs, for garnishing

1 Preheat a 350°F/180°C/Gas 4 oven. Generously grease a large baking dish with the butter or margarine.

~ **VARIATION** ~

Use an equal amount of grapefruit rind and juice to replace the lemon and orange.

2 ▲ Lay the fish fillets skin-side down in the baking dish, in one layer. Sprinkle with salt and pepper.

3 ▲ In a small bowl, combine the lemon and orange rinds and orange juice. Pour the mixture over the fish.

4 Bake until the fish flakes easily when tested with a fork, 15–20 minutes. Transfer the fish to a warmed serving platter.

5 ▲ Strain the juices from the baking dish into a small saucepan. Stir in the cream and chopped basil. Boil until thickened, about 5 minutes.

6 Spoon the citrus sauce over the fish fillets. Garnish with basil sprigs and serve.

Grilled Salmon with Lime Butter (top), Fish Fillets with Citrus Sauce

Sweet and Spicy Salmon Fillets

SERVES 6

2 lb (900 g) salmon fillet, cut in 6 pieces

4 fl oz (125 ml) honey

2 fl oz (65 ml) soy sauce

juice of 1 lime or lemon

1 tbsp sesame oil

¼ tsp crushed dried chilli pepper

¼ tsp crushed black peppercorns

~ **COOK'S TIP** ~

The acid in the citrus juice begins to 'cook' the fish, so grilling on one side only is sufficient.

1 Place the salmon pieces skin-side down in a large baking dish, in one layer.

2 ▲ In a bowl, combine the honey, soy sauce, lime or lemon juice, sesame oil, crushed chilli pepper and peppercorns.

3 ▲ Pour the mixture over the fish. Cover and let marinate 30 minutes.

4 Preheat the grill. Remove the fish from the marinade and arrange on the rack in the grill pan, skin-side down. Grill about 3 in (8 cm) from the heat until the fish flakes easily when tested with a fork, 6–8 minutes.

Cod Steaks with Pepper Crust

SERVES 4

1 tsp each pink, white and green peppercorns

1½ oz (45 g) butter or margarine

4 cod steaks, each 1 in (2.5 cm) thick (about 1 lb/450 g)

salt

4 fl oz (125 ml) fish stock

4 fl oz (125 ml) whipping cream

3 tbsp chopped fresh chives

1 ▼ Wrap the peppercorns in a tea towel or heavy plastic bag and crush with a rolling pin.

2 Melt the butter or margarine in a large frying pan. Remove from the heat. Brush the cod steaks with some of the butter or margarine.

3 ▲ Press the crushed peppercorns onto both sides of the cod steaks. Season with salt.

4 Heat the frying pan. Add the cod steaks and cook over medium-low heat until the fish flakes easily when tested with a fork, about 4 minutes on each side. Transfer the steaks to a warmed serving platter.

5 ▲ Add the stock and cream to the frying pan and bring to the boil, stirring well. Boil until reduced by half, about 5 minutes. Remove from the heat and stir in the chives.

6 Pour the sauce over the fish and serve immediately.

~ **COOK'S TIP** ~

If pink and green peppercorns are not available, use 1½ tsps each of white and black peppercorns.

Sweet and Spicy Salmon Fillets (top), Cod Steaks with Pepper Crust

Fish Fillets with Orange and Tomato Sauce

SERVES 4

3 tbsp plain flour

salt and pepper

4 fillets of firm white fish such as cod,
  sea bass, sole etc (about 1½ lb/700 g)

½ oz (15 g) butter or margarine

2 tbsp olive oil

1 onion, sliced

2 garlic cloves, chopped

¼ tsp ground cumin

1¼ lb (575 g) tomatoes, peeled, seeded
  and chopped, or 14 oz (400 g) canned
  chopped tomatoes

4 fl oz (125 ml) fresh orange juice

orange wedges, for garnishing

1 ▼ Put the flour on a plate and season with salt and pepper. Coat the fish fillets lightly with the seasoned flour, shaking off any excess.

2 Heat the butter or margarine and half the oil in a large frying pan. Add the fish fillets to the pan and cook until golden brown and the flesh flakes easily when tested with a fork, about 3 minutes on each side.

3 ▲ When the fish is cooked, transfer to a warmed serving platter. Cover with foil and keep warm while making the sauce.

4 ▲ Heat the remaining oil in the pan. Add the onion and garlic and cook until softened, about 5 minutes.

5 ▲ Stir in the cumin, tomatoes and orange juice. Bring to the boil and cook until thickened, about 10 minutes, stirring frequently.

6 Garnish the fish with orange wedges. Pass the sauce separately.

Baked Trout

SERVES 4

1 oz (30 g) butter or margarine

1 onion, chopped

1 celery stick, diced

2 slices of fresh bread, cut in ½ in (1 cm) cubes

1 tbsp fresh thyme, or 1 tsp dried thyme

salt and pepper

4 trout, cleaned (each about 8 oz/225 g)

8 rashers of bacon, rinded

celery leaves or parsley, for garnishing

1 Preheat a 450°F/230°C/Gas 8 oven.

2 ▲ Melt the butter or margarine in a frying pan. Add the onion and celery and cook until softened, about 5 minutes. Remove the pan from the heat. Add the bread cubes and thyme, and season with salt and pepper to taste. Stir to mix well.

3 ▲ Season the cavity of each trout with salt and pepper.

4 ▲ Stuff each trout with the bread mixture, dividing it evenly between the fish. If necessary, secure the openings with wooden cocktail sticks.

5 ▼ Wrap 2 bacon rashers around each stuffed trout. Arrange in a baking dish, in one layer.

6 Bake until the fish flakes easily when tested with a fork and the bacon is crisp, 35–40 minutes. Serve garnished with celery leaves or sprigs of parsley.

Seafood and Vegetable Stir-Fry

SERVES 4

1 lb (450 g) rice vermicelli

2 tbsp oil drained from sun-dried
   tomatoes

4 fl oz (125 ml) sun-dried tomatoes
   preserved in oil, drained and sliced

4 spring onions, cut diagonally in ½ in
   (1 cm) lengths

2 large carrots, cut in thin sticks

1 courgette, cut in thin sticks

8 oz (225 g) raw prawns, peeled and
   deveined, or cooked peeled prawns

8 oz (225 g) scallops, shelled

1 in (2.5 cm) piece of fresh root ginger,
   peeled and finely grated

3 tbsp fresh lemon juice

3 tbsp chopped fresh basil, or 1 tsp dried
   basil

salt and pepper

1 ▲ Bring a large saucepan of water
to the boil. Add the rice vermicelli
and cook until tender (check packet
instructions for timing). Drain, rinse
with boiling water, and drain again
thoroughly. Keep warm.

2 ▲ Heat the oil in a wok over high
heat. Add the tomatoes, spring onions
and carrots and stir-fry 5 minutes.

3 ▲ Add the courgette, raw prawns,
scallops and grated ginger. Stir-fry 3
minutes.

4 ▲ Add the lemon juice, basil and
salt and pepper to taste and stir well.
Add the cooked prawns, if using. Stir-
fry until the prawns are all pink and
hot, about 2 more minutes.

5 Serve on the rice vermicelli.

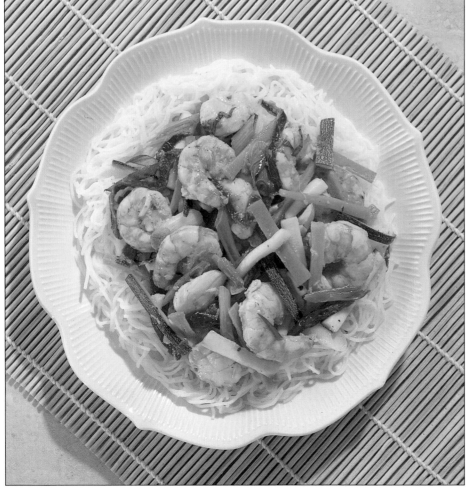

Chunky Seafood Stew

SERVES 6

3 tbsp olive oil

2 large onions, chopped

1 small green pepper, seeded and sliced

3 carrots, chopped

3 garlic cloves, crushed

2 tbsp tomato purée

2 × 14 oz (400 g) cans chopped tomatoes

3 tbsp chopped fresh parsley

1 tsp fresh thyme, or ¼ tsp dried thyme

1 tbsp chopped fresh basil, or 1 tsp dried basil

4 fl oz (125 ml) dry white wine

1 lb (450 g) raw prawns, peeled and deveined, or cooked peeled prawns

3 lb (1.35 kg) mussels or clams (in shells), or a mixture of both, thoroughly cleaned

2 lb (900 g) halibut or other firm, white fish fillets, cut in 2–3 in (5–8 cm) pieces

12 fl oz (375 ml) fish stock or water

salt and pepper

extra chopped fresh herbs, for garnishing

1 ▲ Heat the oil in a flameproof casserole. Add the onions, green pepper, carrots and garlic and cook until tender, about 5 minutes.

2 Add the tomato purée, canned tomatoes, herbs and wine and stir well to combine. Bring to the boil and simmer 20 minutes.

3 ▲ Add the raw prawns, mussels, clams, fish pieces and stock or water. Season with salt and pepper.

4 ▲ Bring back to the boil; then simmer until the prawns turn pink, the fish flakes easily and the mussels and clams open, 5–6 minutes. Add cooked prawns for last 2 minutes.

5 Serve in large soup plates, garnished with chopped herbs.

Special Occasion Seafood Platter

SERVES 6

salt

6 × 1 lb (450 g) lobsters, fresh, frozen and thawed, or cooked

2 lb (900 g) button onions, peeled

2 lb (900 g) small red potatoes

3 dozen small hard-shelled clams, or mussels, thoroughly cleaned

6 sweetcorn cobs, trimmed

8 oz (225 g) butter or margarine

3 tbsp chopped fresh chives

1 Put 1 in (2.5 cm) of salted water in the bottom of a deep pan. Put the fresh lobsters on top. Cooked lobsters should be steamed with 1 in (2.5 cm) of salted water in a separate pan 5 minutes only to heat through.

2 Add the onions and potatoes. Cover the pan tightly and bring the water to the boil.

3 ▲ After 10 minutes, add the clams or mussels and the sweetcorn cobs. Cover again and cook until the lobster shells are red and the potatoes are tender, 15–20 minutes longer.

4 ▲ Meanwhile, in a small saucepan melt the butter or margarine and stir in the chives.

5 Serve the lobsters and clams or mussels with the vegetables, accompanied by the chive butter.

Seafood Kebabs

SERVES 4

16 scallops, shelled, or frozen and thawed

½ tsp ground ginger

1 × 8 oz (225 g) can pineapple chunks in juice, drained and juice reserved

1 small fresh red chilli pepper, seeded and chopped

grated rind and juice of 1 lime or lemon

16 mange-tout

16 cherry tomatoes

8 baby courgettes, halved

1 Put the scallops in a bowl. Add the ginger, the juice from the pineapple, the chilli pepper and lime or lemon rind and juice and stir well. Cover and let marinate at room temperature about 20 minutes, or 2 hours in the refrigerator.

2 Preheat the grill.

3 ▲ Drain the scallops, reserving their marinade. Wrap a mange-tout around a scallop and thread onto 1 of 4 skewers. Thread on a cherry tomato, a piece of courgette, and a piece of pineapple, followed by another mange-tout-wrapped scallop. Repeat until all the ingredients have been used.

4 ▲ Lay the kebabs in the grill pan and brush with the reserved marinade.

5 Grill about 3 in (8 cm) from the heat, brushing frequently with the marinade and turning occasionally, until the scallops are opaque, 4–5 minutes.

6 Serve immediately, on a bed of cooked rice, if wished.

Special Occasion Seafood Platter (top), Seafood Kebabs

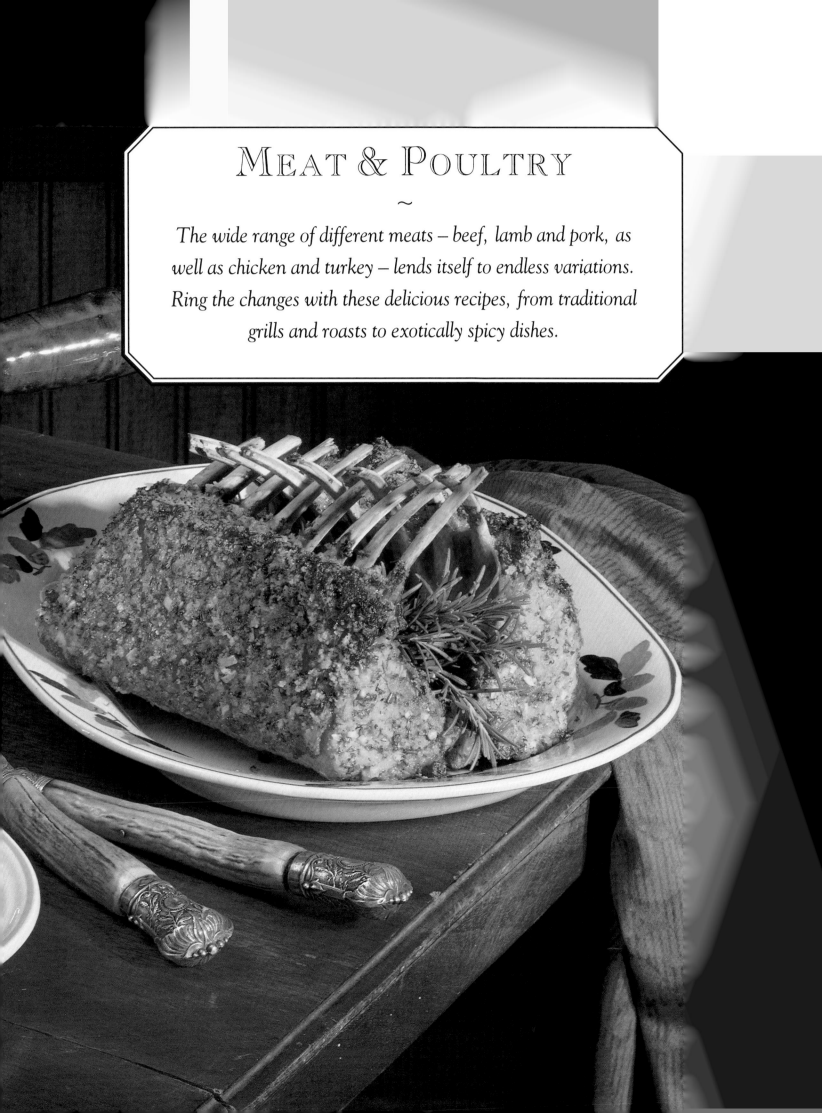

MEAT & POULTRY

~

The wide range of different meats – beef, lamb and pork, as well as chicken and turkey – lends itself to endless variations. Ring the changes with these delicious recipes, from traditional grills and roasts to exotically spicy dishes.

Old-Fashioned Beef Stew

3 tbsp vegetable oil
1 large onion, sliced
2 carrots, chopped
1 celery stick, chopped
1 oz (30 g) plain flour
3 tbsp paprika
2 lb (900 g) braising steak, cubed
2 tbsp tomato purée
8 fl oz (250 ml) red wine
15 fl oz (450 ml) beef stock
1 sprig of fresh thyme, or 1 tsp dried thyme
1 bay leaf
salt and pepper
3 medium potatoes, cut into 1½ in (3 cm) pieces
3 oz (85 g) button mushrooms, quartered

1 Preheat a 375°F/190°C/Gas 5 oven.

2 ▼ Heat half the oil in a large flameproof casserole. Add the onion, carrots and celery and cook until softened, about 5 minutes. Remove the vegetables with a slotted spoon and set aside.

3 ▲ Combine the flour and paprika in a plastic bag. Add the beef cubes and shake to coat them with the seasoned flour.

4 Heat the remaining oil in the casserole. Add the beef cubes and brown well on all sides, about 10 minutes.

5 Return the vegetables to the casserole. Stir in the tomato purée, red wine, stock, herbs and seasoning. Bring to the boil.

6 ▲ Stir in the potatoes. Cover the casserole and transfer it to the oven. Cook 1 hour.

7 Stir in the mushrooms and continue cooking until the beef is very tender, about 30 minutes longer. Discard the bay leaf before serving.

Beef and Vegetable Stir-Fry

SERVES 4

2–3 tsp chilli powder

1 tsp ground cumin

½ tsp dried oregano

salt and pepper

1 lb (450 g) topside of beef, cut into thin strips

2 tbsp vegetable oil

5 spring onions, cut diagonally into 1 in (2.5 cm) lengths

1 small green pepper, seeded and thinly sliced

1 small red pepper, seeded and thinly sliced

1 small yellow pepper, seeded and thinly sliced

4 oz (115 g) baby corn cobs, halved lengthwise, or 8 oz (225 g) canned sweetcorn, drained

4 garlic cloves, crushed

2 tbsp fresh lime or lemon juice

2 tbsp chopped fresh coriander

1 ▼ In a medium bowl, combine the spices, oregano and a little salt and pepper. Rub the mixture into the beef strips.

2 Heat half the oil in a wok or large frying pan over high heat. Add the beef strips and stir-fry until well browned on all sides, 3–4 minutes. Remove the beef from the wok with a slotted spoon and keep hot.

3 ▲ Heat the remaining oil in the wok and add the spring onions, peppers, sweetcorn and garlic. Stir-fry until the vegetables are just tender, about 3 minutes.

4 ▼ Return the beef to the wok and toss briefly to mix with the vegetables and heat it through. Stir in the lime or lemon juice and coriander and serve.

Cheeseburgers with Spicy Avocado Relish

SERVES 6

2 lb (900 g) minced beef

salt and pepper

6 slices of Gruyère or Cheddar cheese

6 hamburger buns with sesame seeds, split and toasted

2 large tomatoes, sliced

FOR THE AVOCADO RELISH

1 large ripe avocado

1 spring onion, chopped

2 tsp fresh lemon juice

1 tsp chilli powder

2 tbsp chopped fresh tomato

1 To make the relish, peel the avocado, discard the stone, and mash the flesh with a fork. Stir in the spring onion, lemon juice, chilli powder, and chopped tomato. Set aside.

2 Preheat the grill.

3 ▼ Handling the beef as little as possible, divide it into 6 equal portions. Shape each portion into a burger ¾ in (2 cm) thick and season.

4 Arrange the burgers on the rack in the grill pan. Grill about 3 in (8 cm) from the heat, 5 minutes on each side for medium-rare, 8 minutes on each side for well-done.

5 ▲ Top each hamburger with a slice of cheese and grill until melted, about 30 seconds.

6 Place a hamburger in each toasted bun. Top with a slice of tomato and a spoonful of avocado relish and serve.

Chilli con Carne

SERVES 8

3 tbsp vegetable oil

1 large onion, chopped

2 lb (900 g) minced beef

4 garlic cloves, crushed

1 tbsp light brown sugar

2–3 tbsp chilli powder

1 tsp ground cumin

1 tsp each salt and pepper

1 × 5 oz (140 g) can tomato purée

8 fl oz (250 ml) beer

15 fl oz (450 ml) fresh tomatoes, blanched, skinned, cooked and sieved

12 oz (350 g) cooked or canned red kidney beans, rinsed and drained

FOR SERVING

1 lb (450 g) spaghetti, broken in half

8 fl oz (250 ml) soured cream

8 oz (225 g) Cheddar or Gruyère cheese, grated

1 Heat the oil in a deep saucepan and cook the onion until softened, about 5 minutes. Add the beef and cook until browned, breaking up the meat with the side of a spoon.

2 ▼ Stir in the garlic, brown sugar, chilli powder, cumin, salt and pepper. Add the tomato purée, beer and sieved tomatoes and stir to mix. Bring to the boil. Reduce the heat, cover, and simmer 50 minutes.

3 ▲ Stir in the kidney beans and simmer 5 minutes longer, uncovered.

4 Meanwhile, cook the spaghetti in a large pot of boiling salted water until just tender (check packet instructions for cooking time). Drain.

5 To serve, put the spaghetti into a warmed bowl. Ladle the chilli over the spaghetti and top with some of the soured cream and grated cheese. Serve the remaining soured cream and cheese separately.

Cheeseburgers with Spicy Avocado Relish (top), Chilli con Carne

Pork with Mustard and Pepper Sauce

SERVES 4

2 pork fillets, each about 12 oz (350 g)

1 oz (30 g) butter or margarine

1 tbsp olive oil

1 tbsp red wine vinegar

1 tbsp whole-grain mustard

3 tbsp whipping cream

1 tbsp green peppercorns in brine, drained

pinch salt

1 Cut the pork fillets across into 1 in (2.5 cm) thick slices.

2 ▼ Heat the butter or margarine and oil in a frying pan. Add the slices of pork and fry until browned and cooked through, 5–8 minutes on each side. Transfer the pork to a warmed serving plate and keep hot.

3 ▼ Add the vinegar and mustard to the pan and cook 1 minute, stirring with a wooden spoon to loosen any particles attached to the bottom.

4 Stir in the cream, peppercorns and salt. Boil 1 minute. Pour the sauce over the pork and serve immediately.

Pork Chops with Apple and Potato

SERVES 6

15 fl oz (450 ml) apple juice

8 oz (225 g) baking potatoes, peeled and cut into ½ in (1 cm) slices

8 oz (225 g) sweet potatoes, or swede, peeled and cut into ½ in (1 cm) slices

1 lb (450 g) apples, peeled, cored, and cut into ½ in (1 cm) slices

salt and pepper

1½ oz (45 g) plain flour

6 pork chops, cut 1 in (2.5 cm) thick, trimmed of excess fat

2 oz (55 g) butter or margarine

3 tbsp vegetable oil

6 fresh sage leaves

1 Preheat a 350°F/180°C/Gas 4 oven. Grease a 13 × 9 in (33 × 23 cm) baking dish.

2 In a small saucepan, bring the apple juice to the boil.

3 ▼ Arrange a row of baking-potato slices at a short end of the prepared dish. Arrange a row of sweet-potato slices next to the first row, slightly overlapping it, and then a row of apple slices. Repeat the alternating overlapping rows to fill the dish. Sprinkle with salt and pepper.

4 Pour the apple juice over the potato and apple slices. Cover the dish with foil and bake 40 minutes.

5 ▲ Meanwhile, season the flour with salt and pepper. Coat the chops with the seasoned flour, shaking off any excess. Melt the butter or margarine with the oil in a frying pan. Fry the chops until well browned, about 5 minutes on each side.

6 Uncover the baking dish. Arrange the chops on top of the potatoes and apples. Put a sage leaf on each chop.

7 Return to the oven, uncovered, and cook until the potatoes and pork chops are tender and most of the liquid is absorbed, about 1 hour.

Pork with Mustard and Pepper Sauce (top), Pork Chops with Apple and Potato

Lamb Kebabs

SERVES 4

1 lb (450 g) boned leg of lamb, cut into 1 in (2.5 cm) cubes

3 medium courgettes, cut into ½ in (1 cm) slices

3 tbsp mint jelly

2 tbsp fresh lemon juice

2 tbsp olive oil

1 tbsp chopped fresh mint

~ **VARIATION** ~

Substitute an equal quantity of orange marmalade for the mint jelly. Instead of fresh mint, use 2 teaspoons of grated orange rind.

---

1 Preheat the grill.

2 Thread the cubes of lamb and slices of courgette alternately onto metal or wooden skewers.

3 ▲ Combine the mint jelly, lemon juice, olive oil and chopped mint in a small saucepan. Stir over low heat until the jelly melts.

4 ▼ Brush the lamb and courgettes with the mint glaze. Lay them on the rack in the grill pan.

5 Cook under the grill, about 3 in (8 cm) from the heat, until browned and cooked to taste, 10–12 minutes, turning the skewers frequently. Serve on a bed of rice, if wished.

Lamb Burgers with Cucumber and Mint

SERVES 4

1½ lb (700 g) minced lamb

1 medium onion, finely chopped

1 tbsp paprika

2 tbsp chopped fresh parsley

2 tbsp chopped fresh mint, or 1 tbsp dried mint

salt and pepper

4 hamburger buns with sesame seeds, split open

FOR THE RELISH

1 large cucumber, thinly sliced

1 small red onion, thinly sliced

3 tbsp fresh lime or lemon juice

2 tbsp vegetable oil

4 tbsp chopped fresh mint, or 2 tbsp dried mint

2 spring onions, finely chopped

1 To make the relish, combine the cucumber, red onion, lime or lemon juice, oil, mint and spring onions in a non-metallic bowl. Cover the mixture and refrigerate at least 2 hours.

2 ▲ In a bowl, combine the lamb, onion, paprika, parsley, mint and a little salt and pepper. Mix thoroughly.

3 Preheat the grill.

4 ▲ Divide the lamb mixture into 4 equal portions and shape each into a burger 1 in (2.5 cm) thick.

5 Grill the burgers, about 3 in (8 cm) from the heat, allowing 5 minutes on each side for medium and 8 minutes on each side for well-done. At the same time, toast the cut surfaces of the buns briefly under the grill.

6 Serve the lamb burgers in the buns, with the cucumber and mint relish.

Lamb Kebabs (top), Lamb Burgers with Cucumber and Mint

Special Lamb Chops

SERVES 4

8 lamb rib chops

salt and pepper

1 egg

1 tsp Dijon mustard

3 tbsp fine dry breadcrumbs

3 tbsp sesame seeds

2 tbsp plain flour

1 oz (30 g) butter or margarine

1 tbsp vegetable oil

1 ▼ If necessary, trim any excess fat from the chops. With a small knife, scrape all the meat and fat off the top 2 in (5 cm) of the bone in each chop. Sprinkle the chops generously with salt and pepper.

2 ▲ In a bowl, beat the egg and mustard together. Pour into a shallow dish. In another dish, mix the breadcrumbs and sesame seeds. Place the flour in a third dish.

3 ▲ Coat each chop with flour, shaking off any excess. Dip in the egg and mustard mixture and then coat with the breadcrumb mixture, pressing it on the meat to get an even coating. Refrigerate 15 minutes.

4 ▲ Heat the butter or margarine and oil in a frying pan. Add the chops and fry over medium heat until crisp and golden and cooked to taste, 4–5 minutes on each side, turning gently with tongs.

Roast Rack of Lamb

Serves 4

2 racks of lamb, each with 8 chops, ends of bones scraped clean
3 tbsp Dijon mustard
1½ tbsp chopped fresh rosemary, or 1 tbsp dried rosemary
salt and pepper
2 oz (55 g) fine dry breadcrumbs
3 tbsp chopped fresh parsley
4 garlic cloves, crushed
2 fl oz (65 ml) olive oil
4 oz (115 g) butter or margarine
8 fl oz (250 ml) chicken stock

1 Preheat a 425°F/220°C/Gas 7 oven.

2 ▲ Brush the meaty side of the racks with the mustard. Sprinkle with the rosemary, salt and pepper.

3 ▲ In a bowl, mix the breadcrumbs with the parsley, garlic and half of the olive oil. Press this mixture evenly over the mustard on the racks of lamb. Wrap the scraped bone ends with foil. Put the racks in a roasting tin.

4 In a small saucepan, melt half the butter or margarine. Stir in the remaining olive oil. Drizzle this mixture over the racks of lamb.

5 Roast the racks of lamb, allowing 40 minutes for medium-rare meat and 50 minutes for medium.

6 Transfer the racks to a warmed serving platter, arranging them so the scraped ends of the bones are interlocked. Cover loosely with foil and set aside.

7 Pour the stock into the roasting tin and bring to the boil, scraping the bottom of the tin with a wooden spoon to mix in all the cooking juices. Remove from the heat and swirl in the remaining butter or margarine. Pour the gravy into a warmed sauceboat.

8 To serve, carve each rack by cutting down between the chop bones, or cut down after every 2 bones for double chops.

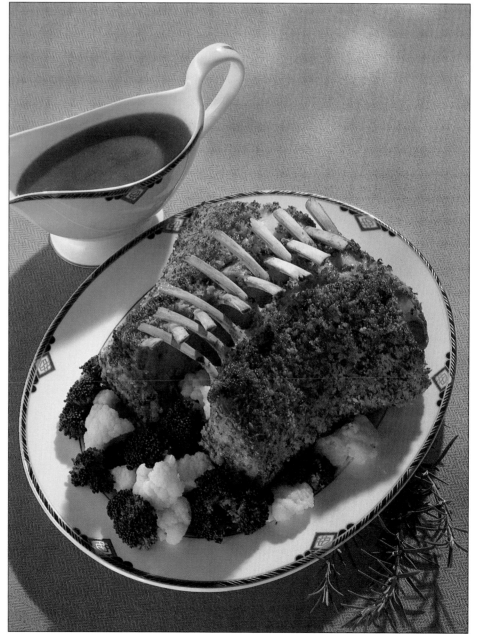

Chicken Breasts with Prunes and Almonds

SERVES 4

1 oz (30 g) butter or margarine
1 tbsp vegetable oil
about 2½ lb (1.2 kg) chicken breast halves
1¼ pt (750 ml) chicken stock
4 oz (115 g) raisins
1 tbsp fresh thyme, or 1 tsp dried thyme
3 fresh sage leaves, chopped
3 tbsp chopped fresh parsley
1 tbsp chopped fresh marjoram, or 1 tsp dried marjoram
2 oz (55 g) fresh breadcrumbs
2 oz (55 g) ground almonds
12 prunes, stoned
4–6 whole cloves
½ tsp ground mace
pinch of saffron strands, crumbled
salt and pepper
1½ oz (45 g) flaked almonds, toasted

1 ▼ Melt the butter or margarine with the oil in a frying pan. Add the chicken and brown 10 minutes, turning once. Transfer the chicken pieces to a large pot.

~ **COOK'S TIP** ~

For ground almonds, chop whole or flaked almonds in a food processor until powdery.

2 ▲ Pour the stock into the pot and bring to the boil. Add all the remaining ingredients, except the toasted almonds, and stir well to mix. Simmer 45 minutes.

3 ▲ With tongs, remove the chicken from the pot and let cool. Bring the cooking liquid back to the boil and boil until well reduced, about 10 minutes, stirring frequently.

4 ▲ Remove the bones from the chicken and return the meat to the sauce. Heat through. Serve sprinkled with the toasted almonds.

Spicy Fried Chicken

SERVES 4

4 fl oz (125 ml) buttermilk
3 lb (1.35 kg) chicken pieces
vegetable oil, for frying
2 oz (55 g) plain flour
1 tbsp paprika
¼ tsp pepper
1 tbsp water

1 ▼ Pour the buttermilk into a large bowl and add the chicken pieces. Stir to coat, then set aside for 5 minutes.

2 Heat ¼ in (5 mm) of oil in a large frying pan over medium-high heat. Do not let the oil overheat.

3 ▲ In a bowl or plastic bag, combine the flour, paprika and pepper. One by one, lift the chicken pieces out of the buttermilk and dip into the flour to coat all over, shaking off any excess.

4 ▼ Add the chicken pieces to the hot oil and fry until lightly browned, about 10 minutes, turning over halfway through cooking time.

5 ▲ Reduce the heat to low and add the water to the frying pan. Cover and cook 30 minutes, turning the pieces over at 10-minute intervals. Uncover the pan and continue cooking until the chicken is very tender and the coating is crisp, about 15 minutes, turning every 5 minutes. Serve hot.

Baby Chickens with Cranberry Sauce

SERVES 4

4 poussins or spring chickens, with giblets, each about 1 lb (450 g)

1½ oz (45 g) butter or margarine

salt and pepper

1 onion, quartered

2 fl oz (65 ml) port

5½ fl oz (170 ml) chicken stock

2 tbsp honey

5 oz (140 g) fresh cranberries

~ **COOK'S TIP** ~

If fresh cranberries are not available, use bottled cranberry sauce and omit the honey.

1 Preheat a 450°F/230°C/Gas 8 oven.

2 ▼ Smear the chickens on all sides with 1 oz (30 g) of the butter or margarine. Arrange them, on their sides, in a roasting tin in which they will fit comfortably. Sprinkle them with salt and pepper. Add the onion quarters to the tin. Chop the giblets and livers and arrange them around the chickens.

3 ▲ Roast 20 minutes, basting often with the melted fat in the tin. Turn the chickens onto their other sides and roast 20 minutes longer, basting often. Turn them breast up and continue roasting until they are cooked through, about 15 minutes. Transfer to a warmed serving dish. Cover with foil and set aside.

4 Skim any fat off the juices in the roasting tin. Put the tin on top of the stove and bring the juices to the boil. Add the port and bring back to the boil, stirring well to dislodge any particles sticking to the bottom of the tin.

5 ▲ Strain the sauce into a small saucepan. Add the stock, bring to the boil, and boil until reduced by half. Stir in the honey and cranberries. Simmer until the cranberries pop, about 3 minutes.

6 Remove the pan from the heat and swirl in the remaining butter or margarine. Season to taste, pour the sauce into a sauceboat and serve with the chickens.

Barbecued Chicken

SERVES 4

3 tbsp vegetable oil
1 large onion, chopped
6 fl oz (175 ml) tomato ketchup
6 fl oz (175 ml) water
2½ tbsp fresh lemon juice
1½ tbsp grated horseradish
1 tbsp light brown sugar
1 tbsp French mustard
3 lb (1.35 kg) chicken pieces

1 Preheat a 350°F/180°C/Gas 4 oven.

2 ▲ Heat 1 tablespoon of the oil in a saucepan. Add the onion and cook until softened, about 5 minutes. Stir in the ketchup, water, lemon juice, horseradish, brown sugar and mustard and bring to the boil. Reduce the heat and simmer the sauce 10 minutes, stirring occasionally.

3 ▲ Heat the remaining oil in a heavy frying pan. Add the chicken pieces and brown on all sides. Drain the chicken pieces on kitchen paper.

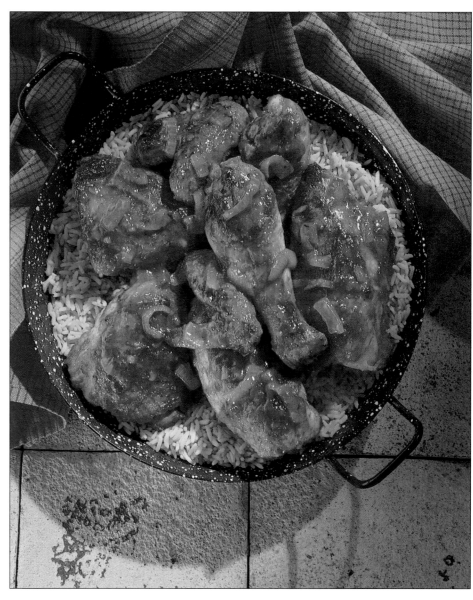

4 ▼ Transfer the chicken pieces to an 11 × 9 in (28 × 23 cm) baking dish and pour the sauce over the top.

5 ▲ Bake until the chicken is cooked and tender, about 1¼ hours, basting occasionally. Alternatively, barbecue over a medium heat for 40–50 minutes, turning once and brushing frequently with the sauce.

Roast Chicken

SERVES 4

1 × 3½ lb (1.6 kg) chicken

2 tbsp clear honey

1 tbsp brandy

1½ tbsp plain flour

5 fl oz (165 ml) chicken stock

FOR THE STUFFING

2 shallots or 1 small onion, chopped

4 rashers of bacon, chopped

1½ oz (45 g) button mushrooms, diced

1 tbsp butter or margarine

2 thick slices of white bread, diced

1 tbsp chopped fresh parsley

salt and pepper

1 ▼ For the stuffing, gently fry the shallots, bacon and mushrooms in a frying pan for 5 minutes. With a slotted spoon, transfer them to a bowl.

2 Pour off all but 2 tablespoons of bacon fat from the pan. Add the butter or margarine to the pan and fry the bread until golden brown. Add the bread to the bacon mixture. Stir in the parsley and salt and pepper to taste. Let cool.

3 Preheat a 350°F/180°C/Gas 4 oven.

4 ▲ Pack the stuffing into the body cavity of the chicken. Truss it with string, or secure with small skewers, to keep it in a neat shape.

5 ▲ Transfer the chicken to a roasting tin which just holds it comfortably.

6 ▲ Mix the honey with the brandy. Brush half of the mixture over the chicken. Roast until the chicken is thoroughly cooked, about 1 hour 20 minutes. Baste the chicken frequently with the remaining honey mixture during roasting.

7 ▲ Transfer the chicken to a warmed serving platter. Cover with foil and set aside.

8 ▲ Strain the cooking juices into a measuring jug. Set aside to let the fat rise to the surface then skim it off.

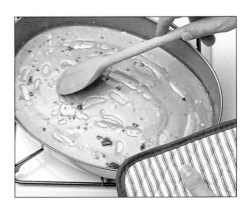

9 ▲ Stir the flour into the sediments in the roasting tin. Add the skimmed juices and the stock. Boil rapidly until the gravy has thickened, stirring constantly.

10 Pour the gravy into a warmed sauceboat and serve with the chicken.

Chicken and Bacon Rolls

SERVES 4

16 rashers of bacon

8 chicken thighs, skin removed

FOR THE MARINADE

finely grated rind and juice of 1 orange

finely grated rind and juice of 1 lime or lemon

5 garlic cloves, crushed

1 tbsp chilli powder

1 tbsp paprika

1 tsp ground cumin

½ tsp dried oregano

1 tbsp olive oil

1 For the marinade, combine the citrus rind and juice, garlic, chilli powder, paprika, cumin, oregano and olive oil in a bowl.

2 ▲ Wrap 2 rashers of bacon around each chicken thigh in a cross shape. Secure with wooden cocktail sticks. Arrange the wrapped chicken thighs in a baking dish.

3 Pour the marinade over the chicken, cover, and let marinate 1 hour at room temperature or several hours in the refrigerator.

4 Preheat a 375°F/190°C/Gas 5 oven.

5 ▼ Put the baking dish in the oven and bake until the chicken is cooked through and the bacon is crisp, about 40 minutes for small thighs and 1 hour for large thighs. Skim excess fat from the sauce before serving. Rice is a good accompaniment because there is plenty of sauce.

Hot and Spicy Chicken Drumsticks

SERVES 4

2 tbsp vegetable oil

8 chicken drumsticks, about 3 lb (1.35 kg)

1 medium onion, chopped

4 fl oz (125 ml) water

3 tbsp Dijon mustard

1 tbsp grated horseradish

1 tbsp Worcestershire sauce

1 tsp light brown sugar

¼ tsp salt

parsley sprigs, for garnishing

1 Heat the oil in a frying pan. Add the chicken drumsticks and brown them on all sides. With a spatula or tongs, remove the drumsticks from the pan and drain on kitchen paper.

2 ▲ Add the onion to the hot oil and cook until softened, about 5 minutes. Return the chicken to the pan. Stir in the water, mustard, horseradish, Worcestershire sauce, brown sugar and salt, and bring to the boil.

3 Reduce the heat to low. Cover the pan and simmer until the chicken is very tender, about 45 minutes, stirring occasionally.

4 ▼ Transfer the drumsticks to a warmed serving dish. Skim any fat off the cooking juices. Pour the juices over the chicken. Garnish with parsley and serve.

Chicken and Bacon Rolls (top), Hot and Spicy Chicken Drumsticks

Turkey Kiev

SERVES 4

4 turkey cutlets (boneless slices of breast), each about 6 oz (175 g)

salt and pepper

4 oz (115 g) butter or margarine, chilled

1 tsp grated orange rind

2 tbsp chopped fresh chives

plain flour, for dredging

3 eggs, beaten

4 oz (115 g) fine dry breadcrumbs

vegetable oil, for frying

orange wedges and parsley, for garnishing

1 ▼ Place each cutlet between 2 sheets of greaseproof paper. With the flat side of a meat mallet, beat until about ¼ in (5 mm) thick, being careful not to split the meat. Remove the greaseproof paper. Sprinkle the cutlets with salt and pepper.

2 ▲ Cut the butter or margarine into 4 finger-shaped pieces. Place a piece crosswise in the middle of a cutlet. Sprinkle with a little orange rind and chives.

3 ▲ Fold in the 2 long sides of the cutlet, then roll up from a short end. Secure with wooden cocktail sticks. Repeat with the remaining cutlets.

4 Dredge each roll lightly with flour, shaking off any excess. Dip in the beaten eggs, then roll in the breadcrumbs to coat evenly. Refrigerate 1 hour to set the breadcrumb coating.

5 Pour enough oil into a frying pan to make a ½ in (1 cm) layer and heat. Add the breaded turkey rolls to the hot oil and fry until crisp and golden on all sides, 15–20 minutes, turning gently with tongs.

6 Remove the cocktail sticks before serving. Garnish with orange wedges and parsley.

Turkey Breasts with Lemon and Sage

SERVES 4

4 turkey cutlets (boneless slices of breast), each about 6 oz (175 g)

salt and pepper

1 tbsp grated lemon rind

1 tbsp chopped fresh sage, or 1 tsp dried sage

2 fl oz (65 ml) fresh lemon juice

6 tbsp vegetable oil

4 oz (115 g) fine dry breadcrumbs

fresh sage leaves, for garnishing

lemon slices, for garnishing

1 Place each cutlet between 2 sheets of greaseproof paper. With the flat side of a meat mallet, beat until about ¼ in (5 mm) thick, being careful not to split the meat. Remove the greaseproof paper. Sprinkle the cutlets with salt and pepper.

2 ▲ In a small bowl, combine the lemon rind, sage, lemon juice and 2 tablespoons of the oil. Stir well to mix.

~ **VARIATION** ~

For a delicious alternative, substitute fresh tarragon leaves for the sage.

3 ▼ Arrange the turkey cutlets, in one layer, in 1 or 2 shallow baking dishes. Divide the lemon mixture evenly between the dishes and rub well into the turkey. Let marinate 20 minutes.

4 ▲ Heat the remaining oil in a frying pan. Dredge the turkey breasts in the breadcrumbs, shaking off the excess. Fry in the hot oil until golden brown, about 2 minutes on each side. Serve garnished with sage leaves and lemon slices.

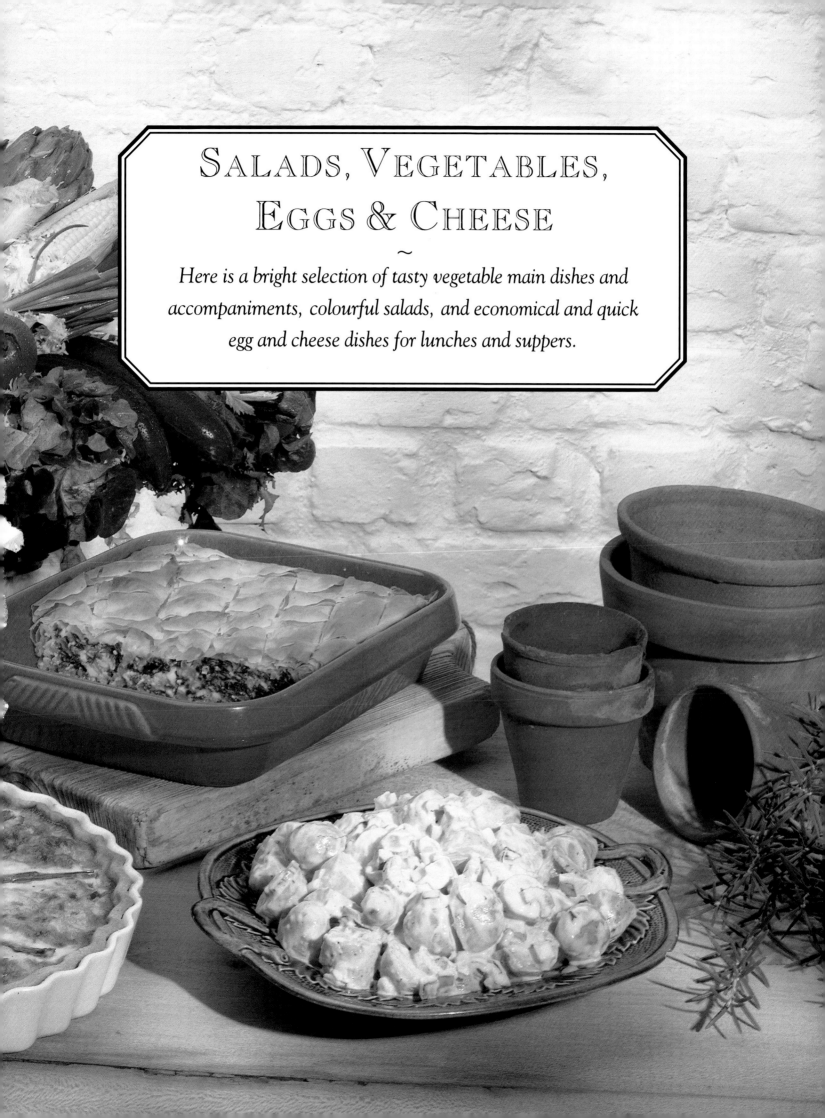

SALADS, VEGETABLES, EGGS & CHEESE

~

Here is a bright selection of tasty vegetable main dishes and accompaniments, colourful salads, and economical and quick egg and cheese dishes for lunches and suppers.

Avocado, Grapefruit and Melon Salad

SERVES 6

1 pink grapefruit
1 yellow grapefruit
1 cantaloup melon
2 large, ripe but firm avocados
2 tbsp fresh lemon juice
2 tbsp vegetable oil
1 tbsp clear honey
3 tbsp chopped fresh mint
salt and pepper
fresh mint leaves, for garnishing

1 ▲ Peel the grapefruit. Cut out the segments, leaving the membranes. Put the segments in a bowl.

2 Cut the melon in half. Remove the seeds and discard them. With a melon baller, scoop out balls from the melon flesh. Add the melon balls to the grapefruit sections. Chill the fruit at least 30 minutes.

3 ▲ Cut the avocados in half and discard the stones. Cut each half in two. Peel off the skin, then cut the flesh into small pieces.

4 ▲ Toss the avocado pieces in the lemon juice. Using a slotted spoon, transfer the avocado to the grapefruit mixture.

5 ▲ For the dressing, whisk the oil into the reserved lemon juice. Stir in the honey, chopped mint and salt and pepper to taste.

6 Pour the dressing over the fruit mixture and toss gently. Garnish with mint leaves and serve immediately.

Sweet and Savoury Salad

SERVES 4

1 medium red onion, thinly sliced into rings
salt and pepper
2 oranges, peeled and cut in segments
1 firm jícama, peeled and cut in matchstick strips, or drained canned water chestnuts
2 heads of radicchio, cored, or 1 head of red leaf lettuce, leaves separated
3 tbsp chopped fresh parsley
3 tbsp chopped fresh basil
1 tbsp white wine vinegar
2 fl oz (65 ml) walnut oil

1 ▲ Put the onion in a colander and sprinkle with 1 teaspoon salt. Let drain 15 minutes.

2 In a mixing bowl combine the orange and jícama or water chestnuts.

3 Spread out the radicchio or lettuce leaves in a large shallow bowl or serving platter.

4 ▲ Rinse the onion and dry on kitchen paper. Toss it with the jícama or water chestnuts and orange.

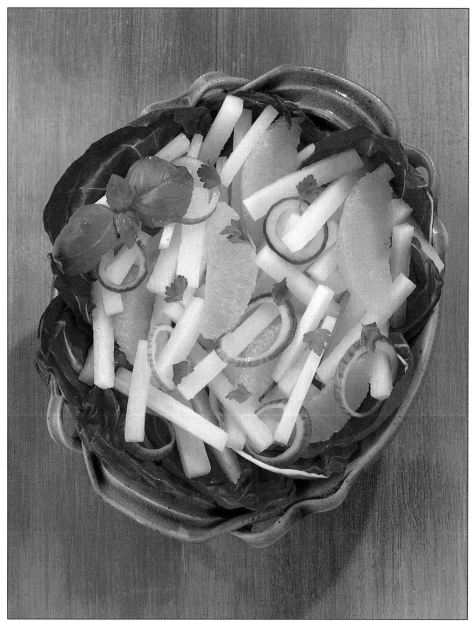

5 ▼ Arrange the jícama or water chestnut, orange and onion mixture on top of the radicchio leaves. Sprinkle with the parsley and basil.

6 ▲ Combine the vinegar, oil and salt and pepper to taste in a screwtop jar. Shake well to combine. Pour the dressing over the salad and serve immediately.

Crispy Coleslaw

Serves 6

12 oz (350 g) green or white cabbage, cut in wedges and cored
4 oz (115 g) red cabbage, cored
3 spring onions, finely chopped
2 medium carrots, grated
1 tsp sugar
2 tbsp fresh lemon juice
2 tsp distilled white vinegar
4 fl oz (125 ml) soured cream
4 fl oz (125 ml) mayonnaise
¾ tsp celery seeds
salt and pepper

1 ▼ Slice the green and red cabbage thinly across the leaves.

2 Place the cabbage in a mixing bowl and add the spring onions and carrots. Toss to combine.

3 In a small bowl, combine the sugar, lemon juice, vinegar, soured cream, mayonnaise and celery seeds.

4 ▲ Pour the mayonnaise dressing over the vegetables. Season with salt and pepper. Stir until well coated. Spoon into a serving bowl.

Tangy Potato Salad

Serves 8

3 lb (1.35 kg) small new potatoes
2 tbsp white wine vinegar
1 tbsp Dijon mustard
3 tbsp vegetable or olive oil
3 oz (85 g) chopped red onion
salt and pepper
4 fl oz (125 ml) mayonnaise
2 tbsp chopped fresh tarragon, or 1½ tsp dried tarragon
1 celery stick, thinly sliced

1 Cook the unpeeled potatoes in boiling salted water until tender, 15–20 minutes. Drain.

2 In a small bowl, mix together the vinegar and mustard until the mustard dissolves. Whisk in the oil.

3 ▲ When the potatoes are cool enough to handle, slice them into a large mixing bowl.

4 ▲ Add the onion to the potatoes and pour the dressing over them. Season, then toss gently to combine. Let stand at least 30 minutes.

5 ▲ Mix together the mayonnaise and tarragon. Gently stir into the potatoes, along with the celery. Taste and adjust the seasoning before serving.

> ~ **VARIATION** ~
>
> Substitute 3 tablespoons dry white wine for the wine vinegar, if preferred. When available, use small red potatoes to give a nice colour to the salad.

Crispy Coleslaw (top), Tangy Potato Salad

Pasta, Olive and Avocado Salad

Serves 6

8 oz (225 g) pasta spirals, or other small pasta shapes

4 oz (115 g) drained canned sweetcorn, or frozen sweetcorn, thawed

½ red pepper, seeded and diced

8 black olives, stoned and sliced

3 spring onions, finely chopped

2 medium avocados

For the dressing

2 sun-dried tomato halves, loose-packed (not preserved in oil)

1½ tbsp balsamic or white wine vinegar

1½ tbsp red wine vinegar

½ garlic clove, crushed

½ tsp salt

5 tbsp olive oil

1 tbsp chopped fresh basil

1 ▼ For the dressing, drop the sun-dried tomatoes into a pan containing 1 in (2.5 cm) of boiling water and simmer until tender, about 3 minutes. Drain and chop finely.

2 ▲ Combine the tomatoes, vinegars, garlic and salt in a food processor. With the machine on, add the oil in a stream. Stir in the basil.

3 Cook the pasta in a large pan of boiling salted water until just tender (check packet instructions for timing). Drain well.

4 ▲ In a large bowl, combine the pasta, sweetcorn, red pepper, olives and spring onions. Add the dressing and toss well together.

5 ▲ Just before serving, peel the avocados and cut the flesh into cubes. Mix gently into the pasta salad and serve at room temperature.

Ham and Bean Salad

SERVES 8

6 oz (175 g) dried black-eyed beans

1 onion

1 carrot

8 oz (225 g) smoked ham, diced

3 medium tomatoes, peeled, seeded and diced

salt and pepper

FOR THE DRESSING

2 garlic cloves, crushed

3 tbsp olive oil

3 tbsp red wine vinegar

2 tbsp vegetable oil

1 tbsp fresh lemon juice

1 tbsp chopped fresh basil, or 1 tsp dried basil

1 tbsp whole-grain mustard

1 tsp soy sauce

½ tsp dried oregano

½ tsp caster sugar

¼ tsp Worcestershire sauce

½ tsp chilli sauce

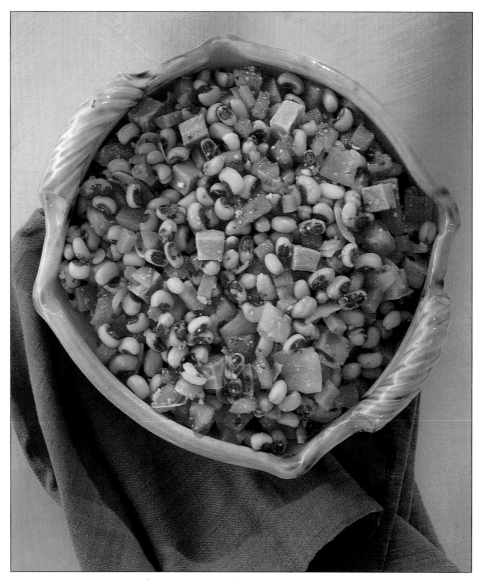

1 Soak the black-eyed beans in water to cover overnight. Drain.

2 ▲ Put the beans in a large saucepan and add the onion and carrot. Cover with fresh cold water and bring to the boil. Lower the heat and simmer until the beans are tender, about 1 hour. Drain, reserving the onion and carrot. Transfer the beans to a salad bowl.

3 ▼ Finely chop the onion and carrot. Toss with the beans. Stir in the ham and tomatoes.

4 For the dressing, combine all the ingredients in a small bowl and whisk to mix.

5 ▲ Pour the dressing over the beans. Season with salt and pepper. Toss to combine.

Scalloped Potatoes

SERVES 6

2½ lb (1.2 kg) potatoes, peeled and cut in ⅛ in (3 mm) slices

salt and pepper

1 large onion, thinly sliced

1 oz (30 g) plain flour

4 oz (115 g) butter or margarine, cut in small pieces

4 oz (115 g) Cheddar cheese, grated

16 fl oz (500 ml) milk

16 fl oz (500 ml) single cream

1 Preheat a 350°F/180°C/Gas 4 oven. Butter a 10 in (25 cm) oval gratin dish.

2 Layer one-quarter of the potato slices in the prepared dish. Season with salt and pepper.

3 ▼ Layer one-quarter of the sliced onion over the potatoes. Sprinkle with one-quarter of the flour and dot with one-quarter of the butter or margarine. Sprinkle with one-quarter of the cheese.

4 Continue layering these ingredients, making 4 layers.

5 ▲ Heat the milk and single cream in a small saucepan. Pour the mixture evenly over the potatoes.

6 Cover the gratin dish with foil. Place it in the oven and bake for 1 hour. Remove the foil and bake until the potatoes are tender and the top is golden, 15–20 minutes longer.

New Potatoes with Savoury Butter

SERVES 6

1¼ lb (575 g) small new potatoes

2 oz (55 g) butter or margarine

3 shallots or 1 small to medium onion, finely chopped

2 garlic cloves, crushed

salt and pepper

1 tsp chopped fresh tarragon

1 tsp chopped fresh chives

1 tsp chopped fresh parsley

1 Bring a saucepan of salted water to the boil. Add the potatoes and cook until just tender, 15–20 minutes. Drain well.

2 ▼ Melt the butter or margarine in a frying pan. Add the shallots or onion and garlic and cook over low heat until softened, about 5 minutes.

3 ▲ Add the potatoes to the pan and stir well to mix with the savoury butter. Season with salt and pepper. Cook, stirring, until the potatoes are heated through.

4 Transfer the potatoes to a warmed serving bowl. Sprinkle with the chopped herbs before serving.

Scalloped Potatoes (top), New Potatoes with Savoury Butter

Broccoli and Cauliflower Bake

SERVES 6

1–1½ lb (450–700 g) broccoli, trimmed

1–1½ lb (450–700 g) cauliflower, trimmed

FOR THE CHEESE SAUCE

3 tbsp butter or margarine

1 oz (30 g) plain flour

12 fl oz (375 ml) milk

3 oz (85 g) Cheddar cheese, grated

⅛ tsp grated nutmeg

salt and pepper

1 Preheat a 300°F/150°C/Gas 2 oven. Butter a 1¾ pt (1 litre) ovenproof bowl or round mould.

2 Break the broccoli into florets. Drop into a pan of boiling salted water and cook 5 minutes. Drain and rinse with cold water to stop the cooking. Drain thoroughly, then spread on kitchen paper to dry.

3 Break the cauliflower into florets. Drop into a pan of boiling salted water and cook 5 minutes. Drain and rinse with cold water. Drain thoroughly, then spread the florets on kitchen paper to dry.

4 ▲ Place a cluster of cauliflower on the bottom of the prepared bowl, stems pointing inwards. Add a layer of broccoli, heads against the side and stems pointing inwards. Fill the centre with smaller florets.

5 ▲ Add another layer of cauliflower florets. Finish with a layer of broccoli.

6 Cover the bowl with buttered foil. Bake until the vegetables are heated through, 10–15 minutes.

7 Meanwhile, for the sauce, melt the butter or margarine in a saucepan. Add the flour and cook 2 minutes, stirring. Stir in the milk. Bring to the boil, stirring constantly, and simmer until thickened, about 5 minutes. Stir in the cheese. Season with the nutmeg and salt and pepper to taste. Keep the sauce warm over a very low heat.

8 ▲ Hold a warmed serving plate over the top of the bowl, turn them over together and lift off the bowl. Serve the moulded vegetables with the cheese sauce.

Green Bean and Red Pepper Stir-Fry

SERVES 4

1 lb (450 g) fine green beans, cut diagonally in 1 in (2.5 cm) lengths

2 tbsp olive oil

1 red pepper, seeded and cut in matchstick strips

½ tsp soy sauce

1 tsp fresh lemon juice

1 Drop the green beans into a pan of boiling salted water and cook 3 minutes. Drain and refresh in cold water. Pat dry with kitchen paper.

2 ▼ Heat the oil in a frying pan. Add the green beans and red pepper and stir-fry until just tender, about 2 minutes.

3 ▲ Remove the pan from the heat and stir in the soy sauce and lemon juice. Transfer the vegetables to a warmed serving dish.

Broccoli and Cauliflower Bake (top), Green Bean and Red Pepper Stir-Fry

Braised Red Cabbage with Apple

SERVES 6

2 lb (900 g) red cabbage, quartered and cored

salt and pepper

2 medium red onions, halved and thinly sliced

2 Red Delicious apples, peeled, cored, halved and thinly sliced

1½ tsp caraway seeds

3 tbsp light brown sugar

3 tbsp red wine vinegar

1 oz (30 g) butter or margarine, diced

1 Preheat a 400°F/200°C/Gas 6 oven.

2 Slice the cabbage quarters thinly across the leaves.

~ **VARIATION** ~

For a sharper flavour, substitute Granny Smith or other tart varieties of eating apple for the Red Delicious apples in this recipe.

3 ▲ Make a layer of one-quarter of the cabbage in a large, deep baking dish. Season with salt and pepper.

4 ▲ Layer one-third of the sliced onions and apples on top of the cabbage. Sprinkle with some of the caraway seeds and 1 tablespoon of the brown sugar.

5 Continue layering until all the ingredients have been used, ending with a layer of cabbage on top.

6 ▲ Pour in the vinegar and dot the top with the butter or margarine. Cover and bake 1 hour.

7 Remove the cover and continue baking until the cabbage is very tender and all the liquid has evaporated, about 30 minutes longer.

Glazed Carrots with Spring Onion

SERVES 6

1 lb (450 g) baby carrots, trimmed and peeled if necessary

1½ oz (45 g) butter or margarine

2 tbsp honey

2 tbsp fresh orange juice

8 oz (225 g) spring onions, cut diagonally into 1 in (2.5 cm) lengths

salt and pepper

1 Cook the carrots in boiling salted water or steam them until just tender, about 10 minutes. Drain if necessary.

2 ▼ In a frying pan, melt the butter or margarine with the honey and orange juice, stirring until the mixture is smooth and well combined.

3 ▲ Add the carrots and spring onions to the pan. Cook over medium heat, stirring occasionally, until the vegetables are heated through and glazed, about 5 minutes. Season with salt and pepper before serving.

Braised Red Cabbage with Apple (top), Glazed Carrots with Spring Onion

Baked Onions with Sun-Dried Tomatoes

Serves 4

1 lb (450 g) button onions
2 tsp chopped fresh rosemary, or ¾ tsp dried rosemary
2 garlic cloves, chopped
1 tbsp chopped fresh parsley
salt and pepper
4 fl oz (125 ml) sun-dried tomatoes in oil, drained and chopped
6 tbsp olive oil
1 tbsp white wine vinegar

1 Preheat a 300°F/150°C/Gas 2 oven. Grease a shallow baking dish.

2 ▼ Drop the onions into a pan of boiling water and cook 5 minutes. Drain in a colander.

3 ▲ Spread the onions in the bottom of the prepared baking dish.

4 ▲ Combine the rosemary, garlic, parsley, salt and pepper and sprinkle over the onions.

5 ▲ Scatter the tomatoes over the onions. Drizzle the olive oil and vinegar on top.

6 Cover with a sheet of foil and bake 45 minutes, basting occasionally. Remove the foil and bake until the onions are golden, about 15 minutes longer.

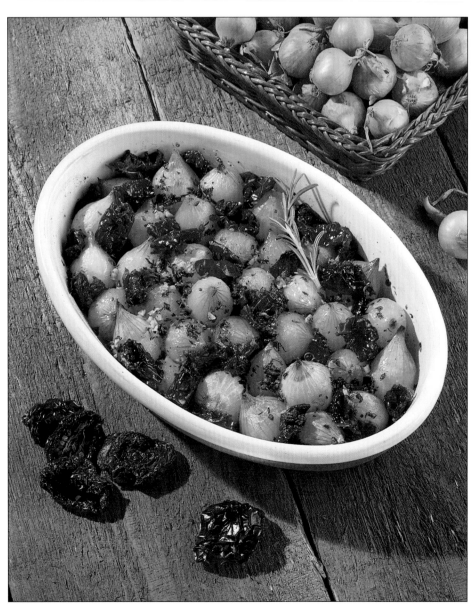

Special Stewed Tomatoes

SERVES 6

2 lb (900 g) very ripe tomatoes, stems
removed

1 oz (30 g) butter or margarine

2 celery sticks, diced

1 small green pepper, seeded and
diced

2 spring onions, finely chopped

salt and pepper

2 tbsp chopped fresh basil

1 Fill a mixing bowl with boiling water and another bowl with iced water. Three or four at a time, drop the tomatoes into the boiling water and leave them 30 seconds.

2 ▲ Remove the tomatoes with a slotted spoon and transfer to the iced water. When they are cool enough to handle, remove the tomatoes from the iced water.

3 ▲ Peel the tomatoes and cut them into wedges.

4 ▼ Heat the butter or margarine in a flameproof casserole or saucepan. Add the celery, green pepper and spring onions and cook until softened, about 5 minutes.

~ **VARIATION** ~

To make stewed tomatoes into a tomato sauce, cook uncovered in a frying pan, stirring occasionally, until thickened to the desired consistency.

5 ▲ Stir in the tomatoes. Cover and cook until the tomatoes are soft but not mushy, 10–15 minutes, stirring occasionally. Season with salt and pepper.

6 Remove the pan from the heat and stir in the basil.

Spanish Omelette

SERVES 4

4 rashers of bacon

3 tbsp olive oil

1 onion, thinly sliced

½ small red pepper, seeded and sliced

½ small green pepper, seeded and sliced

1 large garlic clove, crushed

12 oz (350 g) small potatoes, cooked and sliced

4 eggs

2 tbsp single cream

salt and pepper

1 Preheat a 350°F/180°C/Gas 4 oven.

2 In a heavy 8 in (20 cm) frying pan with an ovenproof handle, fry the bacon until crisp. Drain on kitchen paper.

3 Pour off the bacon fat from the frying pan. Add 1 tablespoon oil to the pan and cook the onion and peppers until softened, about 5 minutes.

4 ▲ Remove the frying pan from the heat and stir in the garlic. Crumble in the bacon. Reserve the mixture in a bowl until needed.

5 ▲ Heat the remaining oil in the frying pan. Lay the potato slices in the bottom of the pan, slightly overlapping. Spoon the bacon, onion, and pepper mixture evenly over the potatoes.

6 In a small bowl, beat together the eggs, cream and salt and pepper to taste.

7 ▲ Pour the egg mixture into the frying pan. Cook over low heat until the egg is set, lifting the edge of the omelette with a knife several times to let the uncooked egg seep down.

8 Transfer the frying pan to the oven to finish cooking the omelette, 5–10 minutes longer. Serve hot or warm, cut into wedges.

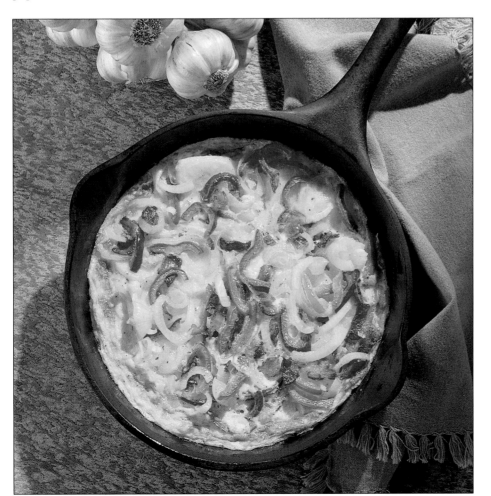

Spinach and Cheese Pie

SERVES 8

3 lb (1.35 kg) fresh spinach leaves, coarse stems removed
2 tbsp olive oil
1 medium onion, finely chopped
2 tbsp chopped fresh oregano, or 1 tsp dried oregano
4 eggs
1 lb (450 g) cottage cheese
6 tbsp freshly grated Parmesan cheese
grated nutmeg
salt and pepper
12 small sheets of frozen filo pastry, thawed
2 oz (55 g) butter or margarine, melted

1 Preheat a 375°F/190°C/Gas 5 oven.

2 ▲ Stack handfuls of spinach leaves, roll them loosely and cut across the leaves into thin ribbons.

3 Heat the oil in a large saucepan. Add the onion and cook until softened, about 5 minutes.

4 Add the spinach and oregano and cook over high heat until most of liquid from the spinach evaporates, about 5 minutes, stirring frequently. Remove from the heat and let cool.

5 Break the eggs into a bowl and beat. Stir in the cottage cheese and Parmesan cheese, and season generously with nutmeg, salt and pepper. Stir in the spinach mixture.

6 ▲ Brush a 13 × 9 in (33 × 23 cm) baking dish with a little butter or margarine. Arrange half the filo sheets in the bottom of the dish to cover evenly and extend about 1 in (2.5 cm) up the sides. Brush with butter.

7 ▲ Ladle in the spinach and cheese filling. Cover with the remaining filo pastry, tucking under the edges neatly.

8 Brush the top with the remaining butter. Score the top with diamond shapes using a sharp knife.

9 Bake until the pastry is golden brown, about 30 minutes. Cut into squares and serve hot.

Asparagus, Sweetcorn and Red Pepper Quiche

Serves 6

8 oz (225 g) fresh asparagus, woody stalks removed

1 oz (30 g) butter or margarine

1 small onion, finely chopped

1 red pepper, seeded and finely chopped

4 oz (115 g) drained canned sweetcorn, or frozen sweetcorn, thawed

2 eggs

8 fl oz (250 ml) single cream

2 oz (55 g) Cheddar cheese, grated

salt and pepper

For the pastry

6½ oz (190 g) plain flour

½ tsp salt

4 oz (115 g) lard or vegetable fat

2–3 tbsp iced water

1 Preheat a 400°F/200°C/Gas 6 oven.

2 For the pastry, sift the flour and salt into a mixing bowl. Using a pastry blender or 2 knives, cut in the fat until the mixture resembles coarse breadcrumbs. Sprinkle in the water, 1 tablespoon at a time, tossing lightly with your fingertips or a fork until the dough forms a ball.

3 ▲ On a lightly floured surface, roll out the dough. Use it to line a 10 in (25 cm) quiche dish or loose-bottomed tart tin, easing the pastry in and being careful not to stretch it. Trim off excess pastry.

4 ▲ Line the pastry case with greaseproof paper and weigh it down with pastry weights or dried beans. Bake 10 minutes. Remove the paper and weights or beans and bake until the pastry is set and beige in colour, about 5 minutes longer. Let cool.

5 Trim the stem ends of 8 of the asparagus spears to make them 4 in (10 cm) in length. Set aside.

6 ▲ Finely chop the asparagus trimmings and any remaining spears. Place in the bottom of the case.

7 ▲ Melt the butter or margarine in a frying pan. Add the onion and red pepper and cook until softened, about 5 minutes. Stir in the sweetcorn and cook 2 minutes longer.

8 Spoon the sweetcorn mixture over the chopped asparagus.

9 ▲ In a small bowl, beat the eggs with the cream. Stir in the cheese and salt and pepper to taste. Pour into the pastry case.

10 ▲ Arrange the reserved asparagus spears like the spokes of a wheel on top of the filling.

11 Bake until the filling is set, 25–30 minutes.

~ **VARIATION** ~

To make individual tarts, roll out the pastry and use to line a 12-cup bun tray. For the filling, cut off and reserve the asparagus tips and chop the tender part of the stalks. Mix the asparagus and the cooked vegetables into the egg mixture with the cheese. Spoon the filling into the pastry cases and bake as directed, decreasing baking time by about 8–10 minutes.

Bread and Cheese Bake

SERVES 4

3 tbsp butter or margarine

1 pt (625 ml) milk

3 eggs, beaten

1½ oz (45 g) Parmesan cheese, freshly grated

⅛ tsp cayenne pepper

salt and pepper

5 large, thick slices of crusty white bread

8 oz (225 g) Cheddar cheese, grated

1 Grease an oval baking dish with the butter or margarine.

2 ▼ In a bowl combine the milk, eggs, 3 tablespoons of the Parmesan cheese, the cayenne and salt and pepper to taste.

3 ▲ Cut the bread slices in half. Arrange 5 of them in the bottom of the prepared dish, overlapping the slices if necessary.

4 ▲ Sprinkle the bread with two-thirds of the Cheddar cheese. Top with the remaining bread.

5 Pour the egg mixture evenly over the bread. Press the bread down gently so that it will absorb the egg mixture. Sprinkle the top evenly with the remaining Parmesan and Cheddar cheeses. Let stand until the bread has absorbed most of the egg mixture, at least 30 minutes.

6 Preheat a 425°F/220°C/Gas 7 oven.

7 Set the baking dish in a roasting tin. Add enough boiling water to the tin to come halfway up the sides of the baking dish.

8 Place in the oven and bake 30 minutes, or until the pudding is lightly set and browned. If the pudding browns too quickly before setting, cover loosely with foil. Serve hot.

Italian Savoury Tarts

MAKES 12–18

2 eggs

3 tbsp whipping cream

3 tbsp crumbled feta cheese

salt and pepper

8 oz (225 g) tomatoes, peeled, seeded and chopped

12 fresh basil leaves, cut in thin ribbons

FOR THE PASTRY

6½ oz (190 g) plain flour

½ tsp salt

4 oz (115 g) lard or vegetable fat

2–3 tbsp iced water

1 Preheat a 400°F/200°C/Gas 6 oven.

2 For the pastry, sift the flour and salt into a mixing bowl. Using a pastry blender or 2 knives, cut in the fat until the mixture resembles coarse breadcrumbs. Sprinkle in the water, 1 tablespoon at a time, tossing lightly with your fingertips or a fork until the pastry forms a ball.

3 ▲ On a lightly floured surface, roll out the pastry thinly. With a fluted 2½ in (6 cm) pastry cutter, cut out 18 rounds. Use the rounds to line 18 cups in a small bun tray. Cut out larger rounds, if necessary, and make fewer tarts.

4 In a bowl, combine the eggs and cream and beat together. Stir in the cheese and salt and pepper to taste.

5 ▼ In a small saucepan, warm the tomatoes with the basil. Drain the tomatoes, then stir them into the egg mixture.

6 ▲ Divide the tomato mixture evenly between the pastry cases. Bake 10 minutes. Reduce the heat to 350°F/180°C/Gas 4 and bake until the filling has set and the pastry is golden brown, about 10 minutes longer. Let cool on a wire rack before serving.

Tangy Bulgur Wheat Salad

SERVES 6

4 oz (115 g) fine bulgur wheat

8 fl oz (250 ml) water

3 oz (85 g) fresh parsley, finely chopped

4 tbsp chopped fresh mint, or 2 tbsp dried mint

2 spring onions, finely chopped

½ small red onion, finely chopped

1 large tomato, chopped

2 fl oz (65 ml) olive oil

3 fl oz (85 ml) fresh lemon juice

salt and pepper

½ head of cos lettuce, leaves separated

1 Place the bulgur wheat in a bowl. Pour the water over the wheat. Let stand until the wheat swells and softens, about 30 minutes.

2 ▲ A handful at a time, squeeze excess water out of the bulgur wheat and put it in a mixing bowl.

3 ▲ Add the parsley, mint, spring onions, red onion and tomato to the bulgur wheat. Stir in the olive oil and lemon juice. Season to taste.

4 Line a large serving platter with the lettuce leaves. Pile the bulgur wheat salad in the middle.

Cheesy Vegetarian Slice

SERVES 6

1¼ pt (750 ml) water

¼ tsp salt

4 oz (115 g) instant polenta

1 egg

6 oz (175 g) Cheddar cheese, grated

1 oz (30 g) butter or margarine

⅛ tsp cayenne pepper

1 Preheat a 350°F/180°C/Gas 4 oven. Grease a 13 × 9 in (33 × 23 cm) baking dish.

2 Put the water and salt in a medium saucepan and bring to the boil.

3 ▲ Stir in the polenta. Reduce the heat to low, cover the pan and cook the polenta until thickened, 5–7 minutes, stirring occasionally.

4 ▲ In a small bowl, beat the egg lightly. Add a large spoonful of the cooked polenta and stir well to mix.

5 Stir the egg mixture into the remaining cooked polenta. Add two-thirds of the cheese, the butter, and the cayenne. Stir over low heat until the cheese melts.

6 ▲ Transfer the mixture to the prepared dish. Sprinkle the remaining cheese over the top. Bake until the cheesy polenta is set and golden on top, 35–40 minutes. Let cool 5 minutes before cutting and serving.

Tangy Bulgur Wheat Salad (top), Cheesy Vegetarian Slice

Fried Rice with Prawns and Asparagus

SERVES 4

3 tbsp vegetable oil

12 oz (350 g) asparagus, cut diagonally into 1 in (2.5 cm) lengths

3 oz (85 g) brown or button mushrooms, sliced

12 oz (350 g) cooked long-grain rice

1 tsp finely grated fresh root ginger

8 oz (225 g) cooked peeled prawns, deveined

4 oz (115 g) canned water chestnuts, drained and sliced

3 tbsp soy sauce

pepper

~ VARIATION ~

Ingredients for fried rice are infinitely variable. Instead of prawns, try scallops or cubes of firm-fleshed fish.

1 ▲ Heat the oil in a wok over high heat. Add the asparagus and mushrooms and stir-fry, 3–4 minutes.

2 ▲ Stir in the rice and ginger. Cook, stirring, until heated through, about 3 minutes.

3 ▲ Add the prawns and stir-fry for 1 minute.

4 ▲ Add the water chestnuts and soy sauce and stir-fry 1 minute longer. Season with pepper and serve.

Saffron Rice

SERVES 6

4 tbsp butter or margarine

⅛ tsp crumbled saffron strands

1 lb (450 g) long-grain rice

1¾ pt (1 litre) chicken stock

½ tsp salt

~ COOK'S TIP ~

If preferred, bring the saffron rice to the boil in a flameproof casserole, then transfer to a preheated 375°F/190°C/Gas 5 oven.

1 Melt the butter or margarine in a large saucepan. Stir in the saffron.

2 ▲ Add the rice and stir to coat all the grains well with the saffron butter.

3 ▼ Stir in the stock and salt. Bring to the boil. Reduce the heat to low, cover and simmer until the rice is tender and all the stock has been absorbed, about 20 minutes.

4 Fluff the rice grains with a fork before serving.

Fried Rice with Prawns and Asparagus (top), Saffron Rice

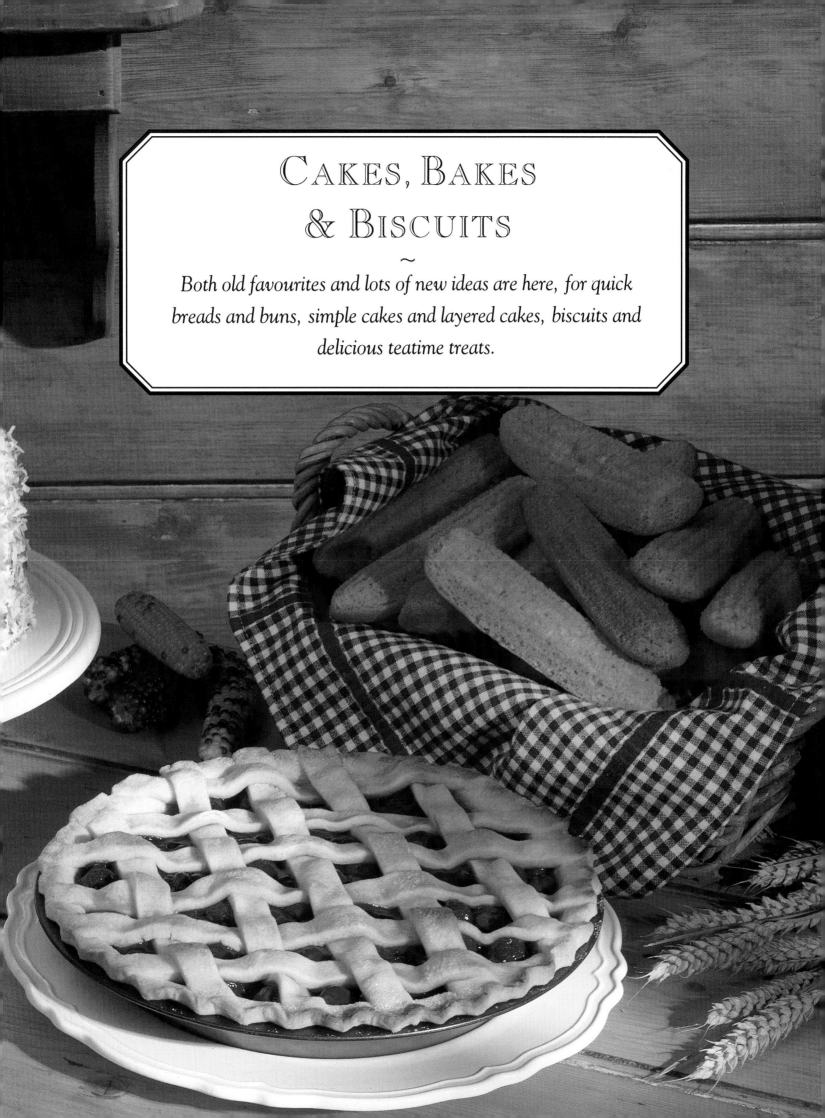

CAKES, BAKES
& BISCUITS

~

*Both old favourites and lots of new ideas are here, for quick
breads and buns, simple cakes and layered cakes, biscuits and
delicious teatime treats.*

Coconut Cake

SERVES 10

6 oz (175 g) icing sugar

4 oz (115 g) plain flour

12 fl oz (375 ml) egg whites (about 12)

1½ tsp cream of tartar

8 oz (225 g) caster sugar

¼ tsp salt

2 tsp almond essence

3½ oz (100 g) desiccated coconut

FOR THE ICING

2 egg whites

4 oz (115 g) caster sugar

¼ tsp salt

2 tbsp cold water

2 tsp almond essence

7 oz (200 g) desiccated coconut, toasted

1 ▲ Preheat a 350°F/180°C/Gas 4 oven. Sift the icing sugar and flour into a bowl. Set aside.

2 With an electric mixer, beat the egg whites with the cream of tartar on medium speed until very thick. Turn the mixer to high speed and beat in the caster sugar, 2 tablespoons at a time, reserving 2 tablespoons.

3 ▲ Continue beating until stiff and glossy. Swiftly beat in the reserved 2 tablespoons of sugar, with the salt and almond essence.

4 ▲ One heaped teaspoon at a time, sprinkle the flour mixture over the meringue, quickly folding until just combined. Fold in the desiccated coconut in 2 batches.

5 ▲ Transfer the cake mixture to an ungreased 10 in (25 cm) non-stick tube tin, and cut gently through the mixture with a metal spatula. Bake until the top of the cake springs back when touched lightly, 30–35 minutes.

6 ▲ As soon as the cake is done, turn the tin upside down and suspend its funnel over the neck of a funnel or bottle. Let cool, about 1 hour.

7 ▲ For the icing, combine the egg whites, sugar, salt and water in a heatproof bowl. Beat with an electric mixer until blended. Set the bowl over a pan of boiling water and continue beating on medium speed until the icing is stiff, about 3 minutes. Remove the pan from the heat and stir in the almond essence.

8 ▲ Unmould the cake onto a serving plate. Spread the icing gently over the top and sides of the cake. Sprinkle with the toasted coconut.

Carrot Cake

SERVES 10

1 lb (450 g) caster sugar

8 fl oz (250 ml) vegetable oil

4 eggs

about 8 oz (225 g) carrots, finely grated

8 oz (225 g) plain flour

1½ tsp bicarbonate of soda

1½ tsp baking powder

1 tsp ground allspice

1 tsp ground cinnamon

FOR THE ICING

8 oz (225 g) icing sugar

8 oz (225 g) cream cheese, at room temperature

2 oz (55 g) butter or margarine, at room temperature

2 tsp vanilla essence

6 oz (175 g) chopped walnuts or pecans

1 Preheat a 375°F/190°C/Gas 5 oven.

2 Butter and flour 2 × 9 in (23 cm) round cake tins.

3 ▲ In a mixing bowl, combine the caster sugar, vegetable oil, eggs, and carrots.

4 Sift the dry ingredients into another bowl. Add in 4 equal batches to the carrot mixture, mixing well after each addition.

5 ▲ Divide the cake mixture evenly between the prepared cake tins. Bake until a skewer inserted in the centre of the cake comes out clean, 35–40 minutes.

6 Let cool in the tins on wire racks for 10 minutes, then unmould the cakes from the tins onto the wire racks and let cool completely.

7 For the icing, combine everything but the nuts in a bowl and beat until smooth.

8 ▲ To assemble, set 1 cake layer on a serving plate and spread with one-third of the icing. Place the second cake layer on top. Spread the remaining icing all over the top and sides of the cake, swirling it to make a decorative finish. Sprinkle the nuts around the top edge.

Apple and Pear Frying-Pan Cake

SERVES 6

1 apple, peeled, cored and thinly sliced

1 pear, peeled, cored and thinly sliced

2 oz (55 g) chopped walnuts

1 tsp ground cinnamon

1 tsp grated nutmeg

3 eggs

3 oz (85 g) plain flour

1 oz (30 g) light brown sugar

6 fl oz (175 ml) milk

1 tsp vanilla essence

2 oz (55 g) butter or margarine

icing sugar, for sprinkling

1 ▲ Preheat a 375°F/190°C/Gas 5 oven. In a mixing bowl, toss together the apple and pear slices, walnuts, cinnamon and nutmeg. Set aside.

2 ▲ With an electric mixer, beat together the eggs, flour, brown sugar, milk and vanilla.

3 ▼ Melt the butter or margarine in a 9–10 in (23–25 cm) ovenproof frying pan (preferably cast iron) over medium heat. Add the apple mixture. Cook until lightly caramelized, about 5 minutes, stirring occasionally.

4 ▲ Pour the mixture over the fruit and nuts. Transfer the frying pan to the oven and bake until the cake is puffy and pulling away from the sides of the pan, about 30 minutes.

5 Sprinkle the cake lightly with icing sugar and serve hot.

Traditional Chocolate Cake

SERVES 10

4 oz (115 g) plain chocolate
12 fl oz (375 ml) milk
7 oz (200 g) light brown sugar
1 egg yolk
9 oz (260 g) plain flour
1 tsp bicarbonate of soda
½ tsp salt
8 oz (225 g) butter or margarine, at room temperature
1 lb (450 g) caster sugar
4 eggs
1 tsp vanilla essence
FOR THE ICING
8 oz (225 g) plain chocolate
¼ tsp salt
6 fl oz (175 ml) soured cream

1 Preheat a 350°F/180°C/Gas 4 oven. Line 2 × 8–9 in (20–23 cm) round cake tins with greaseproof paper.

2 ▲ In a heatproof bowl set over a pan of simmering water, or in a double boiler, combine the chocolate, one-third of the milk, the brown sugar and egg yolk. Cook, stirring, until smooth and thickened. Let cool.

3 ▲ Sift the flour, bicarbonate of soda and salt into a bowl. Set aside.

4 ▲ With an electric mixer, cream the butter or margarine with the caster sugar until light and fluffy. Beat in the whole eggs, one at a time. Mix in the vanilla.

5 On low speed, beat the flour mixture into the butter mixture alternately with the remaining milk, beginning and ending with flour.

6 ▲ Pour in the chocolate mixture and mix until just combined.

7 Divide the cake mixture evenly between the cake tins. Bake until a skewer inserted in the centre comes out clean, 25–30 minutes.

8 Let cool in the tins on wire racks for 10 minutes, then unmould the cakes from the tins onto the wire racks and let cool completely.

9 ▲ For the icing, melt the chocolate in a heatproof bowl set over a pan of hot, not boiling, water, or in the top of a double boiler. Remove the bowl from the heat and stir in the salt and soured cream. Let cool slightly.

10 ▲ Set 1 cake layer on a serving plate and spread with one-third of the icing. Place the second cake layer on top. Spread the remaining icing all over the top and sides of the cake, swirling it to make a decorative finish.

Rich Chocolate Pie

SERVES 8

3 oz (85 g) plain chocolate

2 oz (55 g) butter or margarine

3 tbsp golden syrup

3 eggs, beaten

5 oz (140 g) caster sugar

1 tsp vanilla essence

4 oz (115 g) milk chocolate

16 fl oz (500 ml) whipping cream

FOR THE PASTRY

5½ oz (165 g) plain flour

½ tsp salt

4 oz (115 g) lard or vegetable fat

2–3 tbsp iced water

1 Preheat a 425°F/220°C/Gas 7 oven.

2 For the pastry, sift the flour and salt into a mixing bowl. Using a pastry blender, cut in the fat until the mixture resembles coarse breadcrumbs. Sprinkle in the water, 1 tablespoon at a time. Toss lightly with a fork until the pastry forms a ball.

3 On a lightly floured surface, roll out the pastry. Use to line an 8 or 9 in (20 or 23 cm) pie tin, easing in the pastry and being careful not to stretch it. Make a fluted edge.

4 Using a fork, prick the bottom and sides of the pastry case all over. Bake until lightly browned, 10–15 minutes. Let cool, in the tin, on a wire rack.

5 ▲ In a heatproof bowl set over a pan of simmering water, or in a double boiler, melt the plain chocolate, the butter or margarine and golden syrup. Remove the bowl from the heat and stir in the eggs, sugar and vanilla.

6 Reduce the oven temperature to 350°F/180°C/Gas 4. Pour the chocolate mixture into the case. Bake until the filling is set, 35–40 minutes. Let cool in the tin, set on a rack.

7 ▲ For the decoration, use the heat of your hands to soften the chocolate bar slightly. Draw the blade of a swivel-headed vegetable peeler along the side of the chocolate bar to shave off short, wide curls. Chill the chocolate curls until needed.

8 Before serving, lightly whip the cream until soft peaks form. Using a rubber spatula, spread the cream over the surface of the chocolate filling. Decorate with the chocolate curls.

Creamy Banana Pie

SERVES 6

7 oz (200 g) ginger biscuits, finely crushed

2½ oz (70 g) butter or margarine, melted

½ tsp grated nutmeg or ground cinnamon

6 oz (175 g) ripe bananas, mashed

12 oz (350 g) cream cheese, at room temperature

2 fl oz (65 ml) thick plain yogurt or soured cream

3 tbsp dark rum or 1 tsp vanilla essence

FOR THE TOPPING

8 fl oz (250 ml) whipping cream

3–4 bananas

1 Preheat a 375°F/190°C/Gas 5 oven.

2 ▲ In a mixing bowl, combine the crushed biscuits, butter or margarine and spice. Mix thoroughly with a wooden spoon.

3 ▲ Press the biscuit mixture into a 9 in (23 cm) pie dish, building up thick sides with a neat edge. Bake 5 minutes. Let cool, in the dish.

4 ▼ With an electric mixer, beat the mashed bananas with the cream cheese. Fold in the yogurt or soured cream and rum or vanilla. Spread the filling in the biscuit base. Refrigerate at least 4 hours or overnight.

5 ▲ For the topping, whip the cream until soft peaks form. Spread on the pie filling. Slice the bananas and arrange on top in a decorative pattern.

Cherry Pie

Serves 8

2 lb (900 g) fresh Morello cherries, stoned, or 2 × 1 lb (450 g) cans or jars, drained and stoned

2½ oz (70 g) caster sugar

1 oz (30 g) plain flour

1½ tbsp fresh lemon juice

¼ tsp almond essence

1 oz (30 g) butter or margarine

For the pastry

8 oz (225 g) plain flour

1 tsp salt

6 oz (175 g) lard or vegetable fat

4–5 tbsp iced water

1 For the pastry, sift the flour and salt into a mixing bowl. Using a pastry blender, cut in the fat until the mixture resembles coarse breadcrumbs.

2 ▲ Sprinkle in the water, 1 tablespoon at a time, tossing lightly with your fingertips or a fork until the pastry forms a ball.

3 Divide the pastry in half and shape each half into a ball. On a lightly floured surface, roll out one of the balls to a circle about 12 in (30 cm) in diameter.

4 ▲ Use it to line a 9 in (23 cm) pie tin, easing the pastry in and being careful not to stretch it. With scissors, trim off excess pastry, leaving a ½ in (1 cm) overhang around the pie rim.

5 ▲ Roll out the remaining pastry to ⅛ in (3 mm) thickness. Cut out 11 strips ½ in (1 cm) wide.

6 ▲ In a mixing bowl, combine the cherries, sugar, flour, lemon juice and almond essence. Spoon the mixture into the pastry case and dot with the butter or margarine.

7 ▲ To make the lattice, place 5 of the pastry strips evenly across the filling. Fold every other strip back. Lay the first strip across in the opposite direction. Continue in this pattern, folding back every other strip each time you add a cross strip.

8 ▲ Trim the ends of the lattice strips even with the case overhang. Press together so that the edge rests on the pie-tin rim. With your thumbs, flute the edge. Refrigerate 15 minutes.

9 Preheat a 425°F/220°C/Gas 7 oven.

10 Bake the pie 30 minutes, covering the edge of the pastry case with foil, if necessary, to prevent over-browning. Let cool, in the tin, on a wire rack.

Savoury Sweetcorn Bread

MAKES 9

2 eggs, lightly beaten

8 fl oz (250 ml) buttermilk

4 oz (115 g) plain flour

4 oz (115 g) cornmeal, or polenta

2 tsp baking powder

½ tsp salt

1 tbsp caster sugar

4 oz (115 g) Cheddar cheese, grated

8 oz (225 g) sweetcorn, fresh or frozen and thawed

~ **VARIATION** ~

For a spicy bread, stir 2 tablespoons chopped fresh chilli peppers into the mixture with the cheese and sweetcorn.

1 Preheat a 400°F/200°C/Gas 6 oven. Grease a 9 in (23 cm) square baking tin.

2 Combine the eggs and buttermilk in a small bowl and whisk until well mixed. Set aside.

3 ▼ In another bowl, stir together the flour, cornmeal, baking powder, salt and sugar. Add the egg mixture and stir with a wooden spoon to combine. Stir in the cheese and sweetcorn.

4 ▲ Pour the mixture into the prepared tin. Bake until a skewer inserted in the centre comes out clean, about 25 minutes.

5 Unmould the bread onto a wire rack and let cool. Cut into 3 in (8 cm) squares for serving.

American-Style Corn Sticks

MAKES 6

1 egg

4 fl oz (125 ml) milk

1 tbsp vegetable oil

4 oz (115 g) cornmeal, or polenta

2 oz (55 g) plain flour

2 tsp baking powder

3 tbsp caster sugar

~ **COOK'S TIP** ~

You can also cook the corn sticks in éclair tins or an ordinary bun tray, reducing the cooking time by about 10 minutes.

1 Preheat a 375°F/190°C/Gas 5 oven. Grease a cast iron corn-stick mould.

2 Beat the egg in a small bowl. Stir in the milk and oil. Set aside.

3 ▼ In a mixing bowl, stir together the cornmeal or polenta, flour, baking powder and sugar. Pour in the egg mixture and stir with a wooden spoon to combine.

4 ▲ Spoon the mixture into the prepared mould. Bake until a skewer inserted in the centre of a corn stick comes out clean, about 25 minutes. Let cool in the mould on a wire rack for 10 minutes before unmoulding.

Savoury Sweetcorn Bread (top), American-Style Corn Sticks

Traditional Sugar Biscuits

MAKES 36

12 oz (350 g) plain flour

1 tsp bicarbonate of soda

2 tsp baking powder

¼ tsp grated nutmeg

4 oz (115 g) butter or margarine, at room temperature

8 oz (225 g) caster sugar

½ tsp vanilla essence

1 egg

4 fl oz (125 ml) milk

coloured or demerara sugar, for sprinkling

1 Sift the flour, bicarbonate of soda, baking powder and nutmeg into a small bowl. Set aside.

2 ▲ With an electric mixer, cream the butter or margarine, caster sugar and vanilla together until the mixture is light and fluffy. Add the egg and beat to mix well.

3 ▲ Add the flour mixture alternately with the milk, stirring with a wooden spoon to make a soft dough. Wrap the dough in cling film and refrigerate at least 30 minutes, or overnight.

4 ▲ Preheat a 350°F/180°C/Gas 4 oven. Roll out the dough on a lightly floured surface to ⅛ in (3 mm) thickness. Cut into rounds or other shapes with biscuit cutters.

5 ▲ Transfer the biscuits to ungreased baking trays. Sprinkle each one with coloured or demerara sugar.

6 Bake until golden brown, 10–12 minutes. With a slotted spatula, transfer the biscuits to a wire rack and let cool.

Hazelnut Squares

MAKES 9

2 oz (55 g) plain chocolate

2½ oz (70 g) butter or margarine

8 oz (225 g) caster sugar

2 oz (55 g) plain flour

½ tsp baking powder

2 eggs, beaten

½ tsp vanilla essence

4 oz (115 g) skinned hazelnuts, roughly
   chopped

1 Preheat a 350°F/180°C/Gas 4 oven.
Grease an 8 in (20 cm) square baking
tin.

2 ▲ In a heatproof bowl set over a
pan of barely simmering water, or in a
double boiler, melt the chocolate and
butter or margarine. Remove the bowl
from the heat.

4 ▼ Pour the mixture into the
prepared tin. Bake 10 minutes, then
sprinkle the reserved hazelnuts over
the top. Return to the oven and
continue baking until firm to the
touch, about 25 minutes.

3 ▲ Add the sugar, flour, baking
powder, eggs, vanilla and half the
hazelnuts to the melted mixture and
stir well with a wooden spoon.

5 ▲ Let cool in the tin, set on a wire
rack, for 10 minutes, then unmould
onto the rack and let cool completely.
Cut into squares for serving.

Spicy Pepper Biscuits

MAKES 48

7 oz (200 g) plain flour

2 oz (55 g) cornflour

2 tsp baking powder

½ tsp ground cardamom

½ tsp ground cinnamon

½ tsp grated nutmeg

½ tsp ground ginger

½ tsp ground allspice

½ tsp salt

½ tsp freshly ground black pepper

8 oz (225 g) butter or margarine, at room temperature

3½ oz (100 g) light brown sugar

½ tsp vanilla essence

1 tsp finely grated lemon rind

2 fl oz (65 ml) whipping cream

3 oz (85 g) finely ground almonds

2 tbsp icing sugar

1 Preheat a 350°F/180°C/Gas 4 oven.

2 Sift the flour, cornflour, baking powder, spices, salt and pepper into a bowl. Set aside.

3 With an electric mixer, cream the butter or margarine and brown sugar together until light and fluffy. Beat in the vanilla and lemon rind.

4 ▲ With the mixer on low speed, add the flour mixture alternately with the cream, beginning and ending with flour. Stir in the ground almonds.

5 ▲ Shape the dough into ¾ in (2 cm) balls. Place them on ungreased baking trays about 1 in (2.5 cm) apart. Bake until the biscuits are golden brown underneath, 15–20 minutes.

6 Let the biscuits cool on the baking trays about 1 minute before transferring them to a wire rack to cool completely. Before serving, sprinkle them lightly with icing sugar.

Chocolate and Coconut Slices

MAKES 24

6 oz (175 g) digestive biscuits, crushed

2 oz (55 g) caster sugar

⅛ tsp salt

4 oz (115 g) butter or margarine, melted

3 oz (85 g) desiccated coconut

9 oz (260 g) plain chocolate chips

8 fl oz (250 ml) sweetened condensed milk

4 oz (115 g) chopped walnuts

1 Preheat a 350°F/180°C/Gas 4 oven.

2 ▼ In a bowl, combine the crushed biscuits, sugar, salt and butter or margarine. Press the mixture evenly over the bottom of an ungreased 13 × 9 in (33 × 23 cm) baking dish.

3 ▲ Sprinkle the coconut over the biscuit base, then scatter over the chocolate chips. Pour the condensed milk evenly over the chocolate. Sprinkle the walnuts on top.

4 Bake 30 minutes. Unmould onto a wire rack and let cool, preferably overnight. When cooled, cut into slices.

Spicy Pepper Biscuits (top), Chocolate and Coconut Slices

Ginger Biscuits

MAKES 60

10 oz (300 g) plain flour

1 tsp bicarbonate of soda

1½ tsp ground ginger

¼ tsp ground cinnamon

¼ tsp ground cloves

4 oz (115 g) butter or margarine, at room
  temperature

12 oz (350 g) caster sugar

1 egg, beaten

4 tbsp treacle

1 tsp fresh lemon juice

1   Preheat a 325°F/170°C/Gas 3 oven.
Grease 3–4 baking trays.

2   Sift the flour, bicarbonate of soda
and spices into a small bowl. Set
aside.

3   With an electric mixer, cream the
butter or margarine and two-thirds of
the sugar together.

4 ▲   Stir in the egg, treacle and
lemon juice. Add the flour mixture
and mix in thoroughly with a wooden
spoon to make a soft dough.

5 ▲   Shape the dough into ¾ in
(2 cm) balls. Roll the balls in the
remaining sugar and place about 2 in
(5 cm) apart on the baking trays.

6   Bake until the biscuits are just firm
to the touch, about 12 minutes. With
a slotted spatula, transfer the biscuits
to a wire rack and let cool.

Chocolate-Chip Oat Biscuits

MAKES 60

4 oz (115 g) plain flour

½ tsp bicarbonate of soda

¼ tsp baking powder

¼ tsp salt

4 oz (115 g) butter or margarine, at room
  temperature

4 oz (115 g) caster sugar

3½ oz (100 g) light brown sugar

1 egg

½ tsp vanilla essence

3 oz (85 g) rolled oats

6 oz (170 g) plain chocolate chips

1   Preheat a 350°F/180°C/Gas 4 oven.
Grease 3–4 baking trays.

2   Sift the flour, bicarbonate of soda,
baking powder and salt into a mixing
bowl. Set aside.

3   With an electric mixer, cream the
butter or margarine and sugars
together. Add the egg and vanilla and
beat until light and fluffy.

4 ▲   Add the flour mixture and beat
on low speed until thoroughly
blended. Stir in the rolled oats and
chocolate chips, mixing well with a
wooden spoon. The dough should be
crumbly.

5 ▲   Drop heaped teaspoonfuls onto
the prepared baking trays, spacing the
dough about 1 in (2.5 cm) apart. Bake
until just firm around the edge but still
soft to the touch in the centre, about
15 minutes. With a slotted spatula,
transfer the biscuits to a wire rack and
let cool.

Ginger Biscuits (top), Chocolate-Chip Oat Biscuits

Hot & Cold Desserts

~

*There's always a little space left at the end of a meal for
dessert, particularly if it's rich and creamy, fruity and spiced,
crisp and nutty, icy cold, or, best of all, chocolatey.
You'll find a sweet idea here for every occasion.*

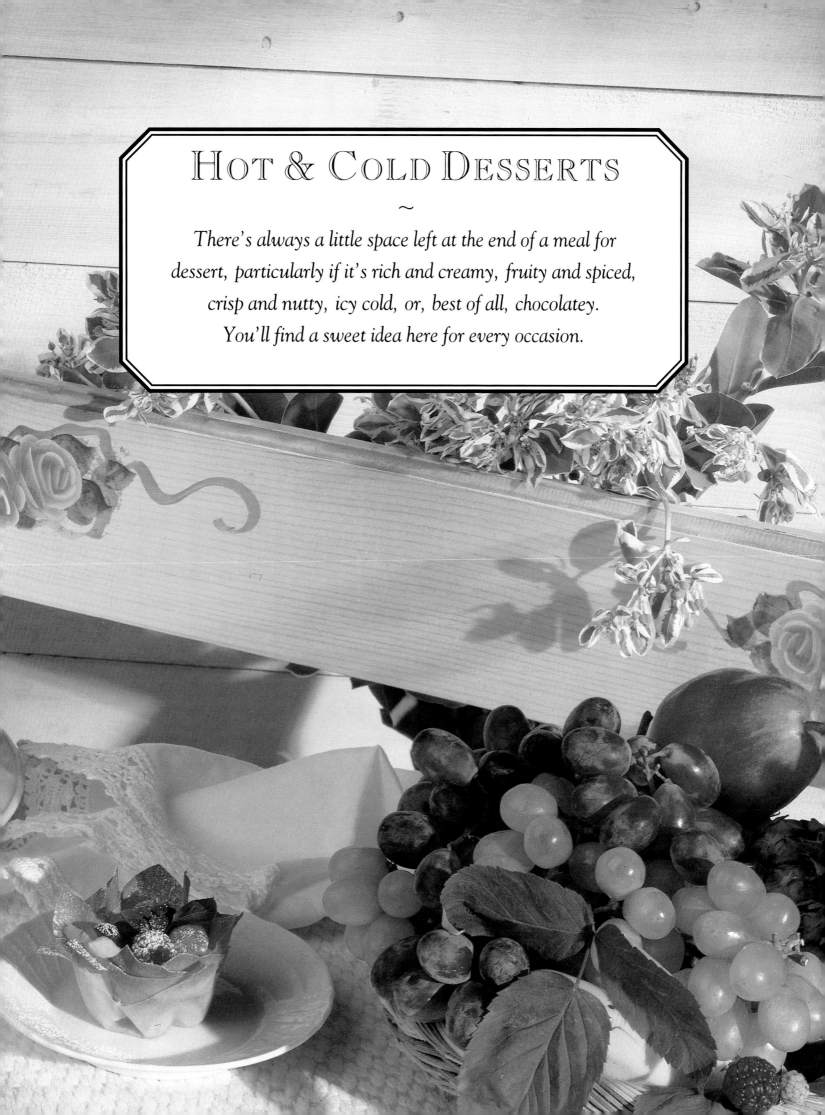

Baked Apples with Caramel Sauce

SERVES 6

3 Granny Smith apples, cored but not peeled

3 Red Delicious apples, cored but not peeled

5 oz (140 g) light brown sugar

6 fl oz (175 ml) water

½ tsp grated nutmeg

¼ tsp freshly ground black pepper

1½ oz (45 g) walnut pieces

1½ oz (45 g) sultanas

2 oz (55 g) butter or margarine, diced

FOR THE CARAMEL SAUCE

½ oz (15 g) butter or margarine

4 fl oz (125 ml) whipping cream

1 Preheat a 375°F/190°C/Gas 5 oven. Grease a baking tin just large enough to hold the apples.

2 ▲ With a small knife, cut at an angle to enlarge the core opening at the stem-end of each apple to about 1 in (2.5 cm) in diameter. (The opening should resemble a funnel in shape.)

~ **VARIATION** ~

Use a mixture of firm red and gold pears instead of the apples, preparing them the same way. Cook for 10 minutes longer.

3 ▲ Arrange the apples in the prepared tin, stem-end up.

4 ▲ In a small saucepan, combine the brown sugar, water, nutmeg and pepper. Bring the mixture to the boil, stirring. Boil for 6 minutes.

5 ▲ Mix together the walnuts and sultanas. Spoon some of the walnut-sultana mixture into the opening in each apple.

6 ▲ Top each apple with some of the diced butter or margarine.

7 ▲ Spoon the brown sugar sauce over and around the apples. Bake, basting occasionally with the sauce, until the apples are just tender, about 50 minutes. Transfer the apples to a serving dish, reserving the brown sugar sauce in the baking tin. Keep the apples warm.

8 ▲ For the caramel sauce, mix the butter or margarine, cream and reserved brown sugar sauce in a saucepan. Bring to the boil, stirring occasionally, and simmer until thickened, about 2 minutes. Let the sauce cool slightly before serving.

Upside-Down Pear Pudding

SERVES 8

2 oz (55 g) plain flour

1 tsp baking powder

¼ tsp salt

7 oz (200 g) plain chocolate

4 oz (115 g) butter or margarine

2 eggs

4 oz (115 g) caster sugar

½ tsp vanilla essence

1 tbsp strong black coffee

1½ oz (45 g) plain chocolate chips

3 oz (85 g) walnuts, chopped

1½ lb (700 g) ripe pears, or 2 × 14 oz (400 g) cans pear quarters, drained

1 Preheat a 375°F/190°C/Gas 5 oven. Grease a 9 in (23 cm) round non-stick baking dish.

2 Sift the flour, baking powder and salt into a small bowl. Set aside.

3 In a heatproof bowl set over a pan of simmering water, or in a double boiler, melt the chocolate and butter or margarine. Remove the bowl from the heat and let cool slightly.

4 ▲ Beat the eggs, sugar, vanilla and coffee into the melted chocolate mixture. Stir in the flour mixture, chocolate chips and walnuts.

5 ▲ If using fresh pears, peel, quarter and core them. Arrange the pear quarters in the prepared baking dish, with the rounded ends against the side of the dish. Pour the pudding mixture evenly over the pears.

6 Bake 1 hour, covering with foil after 30 minutes. Let cool 15 minutes, then hold an upturned plate tightly over the top of the baking dish, invert and unmould. Serve hot.

Baked Pears with Ginger

SERVES 6

6 large firm pears, peeled, cored and sliced lengthwise

3 fl oz (85 ml) honey

2 oz (55 g) light brown sugar

1 tbsp finely grated fresh root ginger

4 fl oz (125 ml) whipping cream

~ **VARIATION** ~

Substitute firm (even under-ripe) peaches for the pears. To peel, dip the peaches in boiling water for about a minute, then slip off the skins. Cook as for pears.

1 ▼ Preheat a 400°F/200°C/Gas 6 oven. Butter a 10 in (25 cm) oval gratin dish or shallow baking dish. Fan the pear slices in a spiral design in the bottom of the baking dish.

2 ▲ In a small bowl, mix together the honey, brown sugar, grated root ginger and cream. Pour this mixture over the pears.

3 Bake until the pears are tender and the top is lightly golden, about 30 minutes. Serve hot.

Upside-Down Pear Pudding (top), Baked Pears with Ginger

Summer Berry Pudding

SERVES 8

8 oz (225 g) plain flour

2 tsp baking powder

½ tsp salt

4 oz (115 g) butter or margarine, at room
temperature

5 oz (140 g) caster sugar

1 egg

½ tsp vanilla essence

6 fl oz (175 ml) milk

10 oz (300 g) blueberries, or blackcurrants

whipped cream, for serving

FOR THE TOPPING

3½ oz (100 g) light brown sugar

2 oz (55 g) plain flour

½ tsp salt

½ tsp ground allspice

2 oz (55 g) butter or margarine

2 tsp milk

1 tsp vanilla essence

1 Preheat a 375°F/190°C/Gas 5 oven. Grease a 9 in (23 cm) round gratin dish or shallow baking dish.

2 Sift the flour, baking powder and salt into a small bowl. Set aside.

3 ▲ With an electric mixer, or using a wooden spoon, cream together the butter or margarine and caster sugar. Beat in the egg and vanilla. Add the flour mixture alternately with the milk, beginning and ending with the flour.

4 ▲ Pour the mixture into the prepared dish. Sprinkle the fruit evenly over the mixture.

5 ▲ For the topping, combine the brown sugar, flour, salt and allspice in a bowl. With a pastry blender, cut in the butter until the mixture resembles coarse breadcrumbs.

6 ▲ Mix together the milk and vanilla. Drizzle over the flour mixture and toss lightly with a fork to mix.

7 Sprinkle the topping over the fruit. Bake until a skewer inserted in the centre comes out clean, about 45 minutes. Serve warm, with whipped cream, if wished.

Peach Cobbler

SERVES 6

about 3 lb (1.35 kg) peaches, peeled and sliced

3 tbsp caster sugar

2 tbsp peach brandy

1 tbsp fresh lemon juice

1 tbsp cornflour

FOR THE TOPPING

4 oz (115 g) plain flour

1½ tsp baking powder

¼ tsp salt

1½ oz (45 g) finely ground almonds

2 oz (55 g) caster sugar

2 oz (55 g) butter or margarine

3 fl oz (85 ml) milk

¼ tsp almond essence

1 Preheat a 425°F/220°C/Gas 7 oven.

2 In a bowl, toss the peaches with the sugar, peach brandy, lemon juice, and cornflour.

3 Spoon the peach mixture into a 3½ pt (2 litre) baking dish.

4 ▲ For the topping, sift the flour, baking powder and salt into a mixing bowl. Stir in the ground almonds and all but 1 tablespoon of the sugar. With 2 knives, or a pastry blender, cut in the butter or margarine until the mixture resembles coarse breadcrumbs.

5 ▼ Add the milk and almond essence and stir until the topping mixture is just combined.

6 ▲ Drop the topping in spoonfuls onto the peaches. Sprinkle with the remaining tablespoon of sugar.

7 Bake until the cobbler topping is browned, 30–35 minutes. Serve hot, with ice cream, if wished.

Rice Pudding with Soft Fruit Sauce

SERVES 6

12 oz (350 g) short-grain rice
11 fl oz (335 ml) milk
⅛ tsp salt
3½ oz (100 g) light brown sugar
1 tsp vanilla essence
2 eggs, beaten
grated rind of 1 lemon
1 tsp fresh lemon juice
1 oz (30 g) butter or margarine
FOR THE SAUCE
5 oz (140 g) strawberries, hulled and quartered
4 oz (115 g) raspberries
4 oz (115 g) caster sugar
grated rind of 1 lemon

1 Preheat a 325°F/170°C/Gas 3 oven. Grease a deep 3½ pt (2 litre) baking dish.

2 ▼ Bring a saucepan of water to the boil. Add the rice and boil 5 minutes. Drain. Transfer the rice to the prepared baking dish.

3 In a bowl, combine the milk, salt, brown sugar, vanilla, eggs and lemon rind and juice. Pour this mixture over the rice and stir well.

4 ▲ Dot the surface of the rice mixture with the butter or margarine. Bake until the rice is cooked and creamy, about 50 minutes.

5 ▲ Meanwhile, for the sauce, combine the fruit and sugar in a small saucepan. Stir over low heat until the sugar dissolves completely and the fruit is becoming pulpy. Transfer to a bowl and stir in the lemon rind. Refrigerate until required.

6 ▲ Remove the rice pudding from the oven. Let cool completely, and serve with the berry sauce.

Surprise Fruit Baskets

SERVES 6

4 large or 8 small sheets of frozen filo pastry, thawed
2½oz (70g) butter or margarine, melted
8floz (250ml) whipping cream
3 tbsp strawberry jam
1 tbsp Cointreau or other orange flavoured liqueur
4oz (115g) seedless black grapes, halved
4oz (115g) seedless white grapes, halved
5oz (140g) fresh pineapple, cubed, or drained canned pineapple chunks
4oz (115g) raspberries
2 tbsp icing sugar
6 sprigs of fresh mint, for garnishing

1 Preheat a 350°F/180°C/Gas 4 oven. Grease 6 cups of a bun tray.

2 ▲ Stack the filo sheets and cut with a sharp knife or scissors into 24 × 4½ in (11 cm) squares.

3 ▲ Lay 4 squares of pastry in each of the 6 greased cups. Press the pastry firmly into the cups, rotating slightly to make star-shaped baskets.

4 ▼ Brush the pastry baskets lightly with butter or margarine. Bake until the pastry is crisp and golden, 5–7 minutes. Let cool on a wire rack.

5 In a bowl, lightly whip the cream until soft peaks form. Gently fold the strawberry jam and Cointreau into the cream.

6 ▲ Just before serving, spoon a little of the cream mixture into each pastry basket. Top with the fruit. Sprinkle with icing sugar and decorate each basket with a small sprig of mint.

Chocolate Cheesecake

SERVES 12

| 1 lb (450 g) plain chocolate, broken into pieces |
| 4 oz (115 g) caster sugar |
| 2 tsp vanilla essence |
| 4 eggs |
| 1½ lb (700 g) cream cheese, at room temperature |
| 2–3 tbsp icing sugar, for decoration |

FOR THE BASE

| 4 oz (115 g) digestive biscuits, crushed |
| 2½ oz (70 g) butter or margarine, melted |
| 2 tbsp grated plain chocolate |
| 1 oz (30 g) caster sugar |

1 ▲ Preheat a 325°F/170°C/Gas 3 oven. Grease a 9–10 in (23–25 cm) springform tin and line the bottom with greased greaseproof paper.

~ VARIATION ~

For an all-chocolate cheesecake, substitute an equal quantity of finely crushed chocolate wafers for the digestive biscuits when preparing the base. For a special topping, pipe whipped cream around the top of the cheesecake and sprinkle with icing sugar.

2 ▲ For the base, mix together the crushed biscuits, melted butter or margarine, grated chocolate and sugar. Pat evenly over the bottom and up the sides of the prepared tin. (The base will be thin.)

3 ▲ In a heatproof bowl set over a pan of barely simmering water, or in a double boiler, melt the chocolate with the caster sugar. Remove the bowl from the heat and stir in the vanilla. Let cool briefly.

4 ▲ In another bowl, beat together the eggs and cream cheese until smooth and well combined. Gently stir in the cooled chocolate mixture until completely blended.

5 ▲ Pour the chocolate filling into the biscuit base. Bake until the filling is set, 45 minutes.

6 ▲ Let cool, in the tin, on a wire rack. Refrigerate at least 12 hours.

7 ▲ Remove the side of the tin and transfer the cheesecake to a serving plate. To decorate, lay a paper doily on the surface of the cake and sift the icing sugar evenly over the doily. With two hands, carefully lift off the doily.

Rich Chocolate Pudding

SERVES 6

3 oz (85 g) plain flour

2 tsp baking powder

⅛ tsp salt

2 oz (55 g) butter or margarine, at room temperature

1 oz (30 g) plain chocolate

4 oz (115 g) caster sugar

3 fl oz (85 ml) milk

¼ tsp vanilla essence

whipped cream, for serving

FOR THE TOPPING

2 tbsp instant coffee

10 fl oz (315 ml) hot water

3½ oz (100 g) dark brown sugar

2½ oz (70 g) caster sugar

2 tbsp unsweetened cocoa powder

1 Preheat a 350°F/180°C/Gas 4 oven. Grease a 9 in (23 cm) square non-stick baking tin.

2 Sift the flour, baking powder and salt into a small bowl. Set aside.

3 In a heatproof bowl set over a pan of simmering water, or in a double boiler, melt the butter or margarine, chocolate and caster sugar, stirring occasionally. Remove the bowl from the heat.

4 ▲ Add the flour mixture and stir well. Stir in the milk and vanilla.

5 ▲ Pour the mixture into the prepared baking tin.

6 For the topping, dissolve the coffee in the water. Let cool.

7 ▲ Mix together the sugars and cocoa powder and sprinkle over the pudding mixture.

8 ▲ Pour the coffee evenly over the surface. Bake 40 minutes. Serve immediately with whipped cream.

Individual Chocolate Soufflés

SERVES 6

2½ oz (70 g) caster sugar

2 oz (55 g) plus 1 tbsp unsweetened
   cocoa powder

3 fl oz (85 ml) cold water

6 egg whites

icing sugar, for dusting

1   Preheat a 375°F/190°C/Gas 5 oven.
Lightly butter 6 individual soufflé
dishes or ramekins. Mix together 1
tablespoon of the sugar and 1
tablespoon of cocoa powder. Sprinkle
this mixture over the bottom and sides
of the dishes and shake out any excess.

2 ▲   In a saucepan, combine the
remaining cocoa powder and the cold
water. Bring to the boil over medium
heat, whisking constantly. Pour into a
mixing bowl.

3 ▲   With an electric mixer, beat the
egg whites until soft peaks form. Add
the remaining sugar and continue
beating until the peaks are stiff.

4 ▼   Add one-quarter of the egg
whites to the chocolate mixture and
stir well to combine. Add the
remaining egg whites and fold gently
but thoroughly, until no streaks of
white are visible.

5 ▲   Divide the chocolate mixture
between the prepared dishes, filling
them to the top. Smooth the surface
with a metal spatula. Run your thumb
around the rim of each dish so the
mixture will not stick when rising.

6   Bake until well risen and set, 14–16
minutes. Dust with icing sugar and
serve immediately.

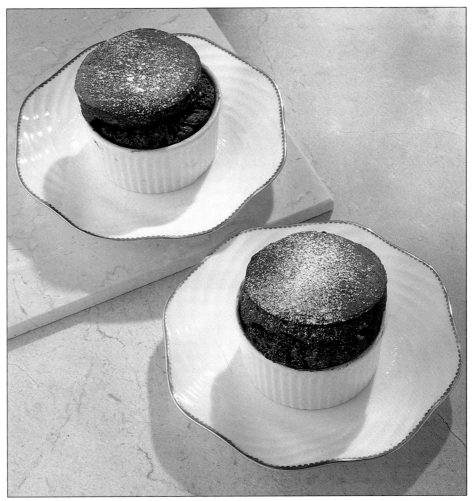

Hazelnut Sundaes with Hot Fudge Sauce

SERVES 8

1 recipe Hazelnut Squares (page 105)

16 fl oz (500 ml) vanilla ice cream

16 fl oz (500 ml) chocolate ripple ice cream

2 oz (55 g) walnuts, chopped

FOR THE HOT FUDGE SAUCE

1½ oz (45 g) butter or margarine

2½ oz (70 g) caster sugar

2 oz (55 g) dark brown sugar

2 oz (55 g) unsweetened cocoa powder

3 fl oz (85 ml) whipping cream

⅛ tsp salt

1 ▼ For the sauce, combine all the ingredients in a saucepan. Cook gently, stirring, until smooth.

2 Put a hazelnut square in each of the 8 glass serving dishes.

3 ▼ Top each serving dish with a scoop of each ice cream. Spoon the hot fudge sauce on top. Sprinkle with chopped walnuts and serve immediately.

Chocolate Biscuit Ice Cream

MAKES 2½ PT (1.5 LITRES)

16 fl oz (500 ml) whipping cream

3 egg yolks

12 fl oz (375 ml) condensed milk

4 tsp vanilla essence

about 12 chocolate sandwich biscuits, coarsely crushed

1 ▲ Line a 9 × 5 in (23 × 13 cm) loaf tin with foil, leaving enough overhang to cover the top.

2 In a mixing bowl, whip the cream until soft peaks form. Set aside.

3 ▼ In another bowl, beat the egg yolks until thick and pale. Stir in the condensed milk and vanilla. Fold in the crushed biscuits and the whipped cream.

4 Pour into the prepared loaf tin. Cover with the foil overhang and freeze until firm, about 6 hours.

5 ▲ To serve, remove the ice cream from the pan and peel off the foil. Cut into thin slices with a sharp knife.

~ COOK'S TIP ~

Buying very fresh eggs from a reputable producer is especially important when using them raw.

Hazelnut Sundaes with Hot Fudge Sauce (top), Chocolate Biscuit Ice Cream

Chocolate Mint Ice Cream Pie

SERVES 8

3 oz (85 g) plain chocolate chips

1½ oz (45 g) butter or margarine

2 oz (55 g) crisped rice cereal

1¾ pt (1 litre) mint-chocolate-chip ice cream

3 oz (85 g) plain chocolate

1 Line a 9 in (23 cm) pie tin with foil. Place a round of greaseproof paper over the foil in the bottom of the tin.

2 In a heatproof bowl set over a pan of barely simmering water, or in a double boiler, melt the chocolate chips and butter or margarine.

3 ▲ Remove the bowl from the heat and gently stir in the cereal, a little at a time. Let cool 5 minutes.

4 ▲ Press the chocolate-cereal mixture evenly over the bottom and up the sides of the prepared tin, forming a ½ in (1 cm) rim. Refrigerate until completely hard.

5 Carefully remove the cereal base from the tin and peel off the foil and greaseproof paper. Return the base to the pie tin.

6 Remove the ice cream from the freezer and let soften 10 minutes.

7 ▼ Spread the ice cream evenly in the crust. Freeze until firm, about 1 hour.

8 For the decoration, use the heat of your hands to soften the chocolate slightly. Draw the blade of a swivel-headed vegetable peeler along the smooth surface of the chocolate to shave off short, wide curls.

Refrigerate the chocolate curls until needed.

9 ▲ Scatter the chocolate curls over the ice cream just before serving.

INDEX

~

ACKNOWLEDGEMENTS

~

For their assistance in the production of this book the publishers wish to thank:

American Country Collections Limited
28 Baker Street
Weybridge, Surrey KT13 8AU

British Gas North Thames
North Thames House
London Road
Staines, Middlesex TW18 4AE

M.C. Typeset Limited
The Barn, Woodbank House
Rochester Road
Wouldham, Kent ME1 3RB

Magimix
115A High Street
Godalming, Surrey GU7 1AQ

Prestige
Prestige House
22–26 High Street
Egham, Surrey TW20 9DU

Staks
24 The Waterglade Centre
The Broadway, Ealing
London W5 2ND